Arts-Based Education to Become Global Citizens

Hiroko Hara

KINSEIDO

Contents

List of Tables v
List of Figures v
Preface vii

Part I: English

1 Introduction: Visual Culture and Technology 2
2 Literacies to Cope with
 Globalization and Digitalization 10
3 Media Education in Japan 14
4 Media Education in Canada 18
5 Critical Thinking 22
6 Decoding: Critical Analysis
 (Gender, Race, and Ethnicity) 26
7 Encoding Stage 1: Employing Active Learning 30
8 Encoding Stage 2: Acquiring Film Techniques 35
9 Encoding Stage 3: Storyboarding 44
10 Encoding Stage 4: Filming and Editing 46
11 Film-Eng Praxis in Practice 49
12 Film Script 61
13 Case Study of the Film Project 68
14 Audience 75
15 Conclusion 81

序文 ………… 89

Part II: Japanese

1 序論：視覚文化と技術 ………… 94
2 グローバル化とデジタル化に対応するリテラシー ………… 101
3 日本におけるメディア教育 ………… 105
4 カナダにおけるメディア教育 ………… 109
5 批判的思考 ………… 113
6 デコーディング：批判的分析（ジェンダー、人種、民族）………… 116
7 エンコーディング第1工程：
　アクティブ・ラーニングの導入 ………… 120
8 エンコーディング第2工程：撮影技術の習得 ………… 125
9 エンコーディング第3工程：絵コンテ作成 ………… 130
10 エンコーディング第4工程：映像撮影と編集 ………… 132
11 フィルム－イング実践 ………… 135
12 映画脚本 ………… 143
13 映画プロジェクト事例研究 ………… 149
14 観客 ………… 155
15 結論 ………… 160

References ………… 167
Index ………… 175
About the Author ………… 178

List of Tables

Table 1. Sample Questionnaire Questions 56
Table 2. Students' Views on the Group Project 58
Table 3. Students' Views on Making a Movie 59

List of Figures

Figure 1. Hand-Held Filming 35
Figure 2. Using a Tripod 36
Figure 3. Panning the Ocean 1 37
Figure 4. Panning the Ocean 2 37
Figure 5. Panning the Ocean 3 37
Figure 6. Tilting a Tall Tree from Top 38
Figure 7. Tilting a Tall Tree to Bottom 38
Figure 8. Wide Shot 38
Figure 9. Medium Shot 39
Figure 10. Close-Up Shot 39
Figure 11. Extreme Close-Up Shot of a Closed Eye 40
Figure 12. Extreme Close-Up Shot of an Opened Eye 40
Figure 13. Two Shot 40
Figure 14. Shooting from above 41
Figure 15. Shooting from below 41
Figure 16. Sample Storyboard 45
Figure 17. Students Forming Groups 50
Figure 18. Students Discussing Ideas 51
Figure 19. Storyboarding 52
Figure 20. Students Discussing their Storyboard 52
Figure 21. Students Coloring their Storyboard 53
Figure 22. Completed Storyboard (Page 1) 53
Figure 23. Completed Storyboard (Page 2) 54

Figure 24. Presenting with the Digital Projection System   54
Figure 25. Students Presenting their Storyboard   55
Figure 26. Presenters and Viewers   55
Figure 27. Still 1 from *Yugen*   61
Figure 28. Still 2 from *Yugen*   63
Figure 29. Still 3 from *Yugen*   64
Figure 30. Still 4 from *Yugen*   66
Figure 31. Still 5 from *Yugen*   67
Figure 32. Seminar Members Creating Rhythm   73

Preface

It has been five years since I returned to my homeland Japan. I have been practicing global citizenship by living in various places such as Canada, the United States, and Japan. What I believe now is that practicing global citizenship requires the language skills, the will to communicate with people from diverse backgrounds, and the courage to express oneself.

English is essential for us living in the 21st century, for it is a global language, namely, a key communication tool in this globalizing world. At the same time, however, having a good command of the Japanese language is also important for learners of English situated in Japan. Therefore, this book is composed of two parts—English and Japanese, that is, bilingual.

When I was a graduate student working on my research project, I met a person who immigrated to Japan from Cambodia due to the political chaos in the country. This person told me to not forget my roots and to cherish the language and culture of my native country.

Back in Japan, I started to face the culture once again. In her book entitled *Infinity Net*, Yayoi Kusama (2011) articulates the significance of expressing herself in Japanese, which she calls the "rediscovered first language":

> Since moving to the USA in 1957 I had fought my way through with my art, as a standard bearer for the international avant-garde, dashing about the globe; during that time, of course, I communicated predominantly in English, did most of my thinking in English, and

even muttered to myself in English. Then, returning to Japan, I met up again with my native language. By writing novels and poems in Japanese, I was able to shine light on a different facet of myself, one that I could not reach with plastic arts. This allowed me to cultivate new spheres of self and reorient my soul. (p. 206)

Similarly, I decided to re-examine what constitutes Japan with my own eyes. Incorporating the Japanese translation in this book is my attempt as such.

When I think about my own identity, I always come to realize that it is impossible to be away from transnationality and transculturality. I believe there exists something in-between English and Japanese, which is difficult to express. But I found out that a combination of image, sound, and word could broaden our horizons and help us see in-between elements. Hence, as a means to show the thing that cannot be expressed easily, I apply filmmaking.

What makes it possible to express something in-between? That is a question I have had in mind for years. However, based on my experience of having studied at the Gulf Islands Film and Television School and taught film techniques at the University of British Columbia, Canada, I can say that expression through a merger of image, sound, and word in film is very helpful for me as a global citizen immersed in various "trans" elements.

Having worked in Japanese higher education, I am convinced that the young, digital generation in Japan have the potential to become vigorous global citizens with a high level of language competence and advanced ICT skills. I hope this book serves as a textbook showing how to transform oneself into an active global citizen.

This project would not have been possible without the encouragement of Professor Atsuko Hayakawa and Dr. Jennifer Chan, whom I respect from my heart. They are role models of mine and I hope to convey important messages as they have been continuously doing so. In addition, I am truly thankful to Dr. Noriko Inuzuka for providing me with a great deal of helpful advice. I am also grateful to Professor Masayuki Okahara and Dr. Yasutsugu Ogura for inspiring me to practice arts-based education and research. Moreover, I appreciate the kind consultation offered by Mr. Hiroshi Yokoyama of Kinseido for publishing this book. Last but not least, I wish to thank all the precious students of mine, who participated in this project. Especially, I am very fortunate to have made a film together with the talented seminar members—Ayano, Kanako, Kasumi, and Risako, and obtained valuable comments about the produced film from the study-abroad participants—Mayu, Miu, Mizuki, Reina, and Rina. These thoughtful and creative students spur me to cut my way as an educator/filmmaker/researcher. Girls and boys, fly out locally and globally, and create new values verbally and visually!

H.H.
September 2017

Part I: English

Roots to Routes

1
Introduction: Visual Culture and Technology

Apprendre à marcher de nouveau
Learning how to walk anew ...

cette image que je suis
this image that I am

entendre
avec l'oreille de l'autre
hear
with the other's ear

savoir par le non-savoir
know through nonknowing

l'entrée en soi ouvre sur l'autre
moving into oneself opens onto the other ...
         (Trinh T. Minh-ha, 2013, p. 177; original emphasis)

With the technological advancement, digital video cameras have replaced the earlier cameras such as 8mm and 16mm, and the new types of image storage (e.g., DVDs, USB memory sticks, etc.) are substituted for reel films. These technological inventions have become mass products. More people now own digital video cameras, make movies, and upload their works onto information-sharing websites. According to Nicholas

Mirzoeff (1998), from the movement as such emerged "visual culture," and suggests that its expansion is inseparable from the development of "visual technology." By "visual technology," Mirzoeff means "... any form of apparatus designed either to be looked at or to enhance natural vision, from oil painting to television and the Internet" (1998, p. 3).

We can see the impact of visual culture and technology on the young generation in Japan. The National Institution for Youth Education (2015) shows that 75% of high school students spend time (ranging from 1 hour to more than 6 hours) on weekdays in going on the Internet and using social networking sites (SNS) such as Facebook, LINE, and Twitter. Hence, it is reasonable to call these youngsters in Japan the "digital generation." With the diffusion of cellphones ("smartphones" in the case of Japan), people use them for photographing and recording, and share their pictures and videos online. Videos recorded by cellphones are called "cellphilms," and scholars have recently paid attention to this new digital expression as an emerging research subject (e.g., Mitchell, 2016; Moletsane, Mitchell, & Lewin, 2015). Similarly, having smartphones handy, young people in Japan are free to create "cellphilms"; they are at the forefront of the era in which visual culture and technology are making remarkable advances.

Taking account of the young digital generation as such, the Ministry of Education, Culture, Sports, Science and Technology, Japan (MEXT) released a document titled *The Second Basic Plan for the Promotion of Education* in June 2013. In this plan, MEXT indicates that "... in a globalizing industrialized society, English and media literacy are becoming indispensable" (2013a). MEXT thus specifies the two components— "English and media literacy"—as essential for the future generation. In this book, I suggest that incorporating the arts in education is necessary in order to obtain the two. Indeed, in their report called *White Paper on*

Education, Culture, Sports, Science and Technology, MEXT asserts the importance of the arts as follows:

> By 2020, one goal is to make Japan an attractive country that is rooted in the arts and culture, and a hub for international cultural exchange that will attract artists, young people, cultural figures, and scholars to visit Japan. The other goal is to present Japan to the world as a nation rooted in the arts and culture where new values are created, and as a new model for the mature society supported by the arts and culture. (2013b)

As described here, it is now believed that the arts hold the key to the advent and spread of alternative views in the coming future.

This is a new trend resulting from the contribution of researchers who advocate attaching importance to the arts in education (e.g., Dewey, 1934; Eisner, 1972; Frank, 1966; Lewis, 1976). While science forges ahead in society, John Dewey (1934) urges people to take notice of the significance of art distinct from science: "Art is a mode of prediction not found in charts and statistics, and it insinuates possibilities of human relations not to be found in rule and precept, admonition and administration" (p. 349). Lawrence Frank (1966) also regards art as pivotal in science-driven society, and argues that "[t]he arts still wait for full acceptance in educational programs in which they are indispensable and urgently needed" (p. 459).

Highlighting the importance of integrating the arts in education, scholars have long investigated the root of the problem that the arts are overlooked in not only school but also society as a whole. Dewey offers a useful analysis in which he directs his attention to dichotomization:

> The opposition that now exists between the spiritual and ideal

> elements of our historic heritage and the structure of physical nature that is disclosed by science, is the ultimate source of the dualisms formulated by philosophy since Descartes and Locke. (1934, p. 338)

Dewey thus reveals the maintenance of the binary system, which leads to the division between science and art. In relation to the dichotomy described by Dewey, Elliot Eisner (1972) points out the impact of Greek philosophy: "Ever since Plato distinguished between the work of the head and the work of the hand, assigning the former to the higher levels of goodness than the latter, there has been little question about which realm the arts occupied" (p. 262). Regarding the binary structure as such, Hilda Lewis (1976) explains how to transgress it:

> What I am suggesting is that we view the arts, the humanities, and the sciences as complementary manifestations of how people deal with the natural and social environment, that we dismantle the wall separating the affective from the cognitive, that we reform the curriculum by unifying the teaching of the arts around the basic processes that bring together the arts and other disciplines. (p. 168)

Here Lewis denotes the relevance between the disciplinary boundaries and the dichotomy such as "affect/cognition," and indicates the need to import a new framework into the curriculum, which keeps all the subjects harmonious.

Indeed, scholars have presented models of incorporating various forms of art into education and research, which are called "arts-based" (e.g., Barone & Eisner, 2012; Eisner, 2002; Hickman, 2007; Leavy, 2015; Siegesmund & Cahnmann-Taylor, 2008). Eisner (2002) emphasizes the significance of the arts as follows:

> There is, in the arts, more than one interpretation to a musical score, more than one way to describe a painting or a sculpture, more than one appropriate form for a dance performance, more than one meaning for a poetic rendering of a person or a situation. In the arts diversity and variability are made central. This is one lesson that education can learn from the arts. (p. 197)

In this way, Eisner promotes utilizing the arts for education and research, and asserts that multifarious perspectives arise from it. Patricia Leavy (2015) illustrates the characteristics of this new methodology:

> *Arts-based research practices* are a set of methodological tools used by researchers across the disciplines during all phases of social research, including data generation, analysis, interpretation, and representation. These emerging tools adapt the tenets of the creative arts in order to address social research questions in holistic and engaged ways in which theory and practice are intertwined.
> (p. 4; original emphasis)

Hence, arts-based methods are useful for not only transgressing the previously described binaries but also blurring the boundary between "theory" and "practice." Tom Barone and Elliot Eisner (2012) attest that arts-based approaches embrace great potentialities:

> Instead of contributing to the stability of prevailing assumptions about these [social and cultural] phenomena by … reinforcing the conventional way of viewing them, the arts based researcher may *persuade* readers or percipients of the work (including the artist herself) to revisit the world from a different direction, seeing it through fresh eyes, and thereby calling into question a singular, orthodox point of view (POV). (p. 16; original emphasis)

What Barone and Eisner suggest here is that arts-based practices abolish the traditional manner of generating single, absolute knowledge, and instead, offer the good opportunity to be critical about what is taken for granted.

Influenced by these scholars and the current digital wave, I intend to offer an example of arts-based practices and explore the potential of applying the arts in the classroom. The arts include various artistic forms—painting, sculpting, singing, playing musical instruments, theatre, performance, blogging, photographing, filming, and so forth. In this book, I focus on filming and seek to illustrate the significance of incorporating it into the teaching and learning environment. For this purpose, I introduce the Film-Eng praxis, which involves producing a certain visual expression (e.g., storyboarding and filming) and using English in the classroom. "Film-Eng" is a cross between "Filming" and "English"; it is the newly coined word which this book presents. I consider this praxis as an art form and artistic practice, namely, an arts-based approach, and argue that it needs to be acknowledged and practiced in various educational settings. The terms "filming" and "filmmaking" are interchangeable in this book. Creative expression through the Film-Eng praxis cultivates the English language skills and critical media literacy, which leads us to elevate the skills of "decoding" and "encoding." In decoding, we interpret messages constructed and distributed by media. In encoding, we apply languages (e.g., English and Japanese) to express ourselves and convey our own messages.

This book shows how the Film-Eng praxis can be implemented in the classroom and suggests this new educational practice benefits learners of English as a Foreign Language (EFL) situated in Japan. The book consists of two parts—Part I: English and Part II: Japanese, and each part is composed of fifteen units. Unit 2 introduces literacies (including critical media literacy) necessary to cope with accelerated globalization and digitalization. This leads to the discussion of how media education is conceptualized in Japan and Canada in Units 3 and 4. Unit 5 shows theoretical bases behind the educational policies of the two countries. Referring to Stuart Hall, I explore what decoding means, and present a model of analyzing representations of gender, race, and ethnicity from a critical perspective in Unit 6. Units 7 to 10 describe the following four processes required for encoding: 1) active learning; 2) film techniques; 3) storyboarding; and 4) filming and editing. In Unit 11, I elucidate the Film-Eng praxis, which can be applied to college classes, and introduce the voices of the students who actually carried out the praxis. Some students of mine created a short film entitled *Yugen* and its script is available in Unit 12. Unit 13 explains the concept underlying the film and what the students as filmmakers intended to tell the viewers. Drawing on the comments of the students who watched *Yugen*, I discuss various ways of decoding done by the audiences in Unit 14. Lastly, the concluding unit offers a summary of findings, discussion, and implications of the Film-Eng praxis as an arts-based approach. In this book, all the students appear under the pseudonym they chose for themselves in order to ensure confidentiality.

The Film-Eng praxis holds multiple possibilities for both educators and learners, if it is practiced properly. This book will make theoretical, methodological, and policy contributions to media education, arts-based education, and educational policy studies. Theoretically, my research furthers our understanding of the relationships between decoding (receiving and interpreting) and encoding (creating and conveying) messages. Methodologically, I bring a novel model of combining qualitative and visual research methods to support my argument of the great potential of the Film-Eng praxis as an arts-based approach. At the policy level, the book of mine points out the gap between discourse and practice of education for promoting critical media literacy, which can inform similar project conceptualization and implementation in other educational institutions.

2
Literacies to Cope with Globalization and Digitalization

A considerable number of studies on literacy have been done by scholars in various academic disciplines such as education, linguistics, psychology, anthropology, sociology, and history. This book mainly focuses on two types of literacy—English and critical media literacy. First of all, English is becoming more and more important in Japanese society on the whole. In particular, the English language communication skills are essential. This is apparent from the Prime Minister of Japan and His Cabinet's *Japan Revitalization Strategy* aiming to "… facilitate practical English language education …" (2014, p. 72).

The shift in education as such is due to the rise of English as a global language. It is the fact that many university students in Japan take English classes required for graduation. Indeed, as seen in their *English Education Reform Plan Corresponding to Globalization*, MEXT strives for "… the full scale development of new English education in Japan …" (2013c) by accelerating English language education in the elementary, junior high, and high school levels. Regarding this alternative language education, MEXT gives a full account of their plan:

> As the new style of English language education, the plan surely promotes English communication skills through (1) English language activities in the third and fourth grade and English as a subject in the fifth and sixth grade in elementary school; (2) upgrade goals

and content of English language education by conducting classes in English in junior high school, and focusing on presentations and debates in high school; (3) establish consistent learning goals through elementary, junior high and high school. (2013b)

In sum, one type of literacy needed for the 21st century is to be able to express ideas in English, and the English language skills are indispensable for the young generation living in Japan.

Next, the other type of literacy to be addressed in this book is critical media literacy. Along with the progress of visual culture and technology, the concept of literacy has shifted. Using the term "multiliteracies," Michal Tannenbaum and Adi Goldstein (2005) argue that literacy is "… related not only to the written or even to the oral language, but also to visual, audial, spatial, behavioral, and other modes of designing meanings" (p. 124). Skills needed for coping with the advancement of technology have been discussed using various terms—"media literacy," "visual literacy" (Chauvin, 2003); "information literacy" (Ragains, 2006); "visual media literacy" (Duffelmeyer, 2004); and "digital literacy" (Tyner, 2003). According to B. A. Chauvin (2003), regarding media literacy and visual literacy, there have been debates among scholars whether these two are identical or not. Chauvin presents the difference between them; media literacy focuses on skills (i.e., evaluation and communication) relevant to the mass media, while visual literacy includes the ability to create a message.

Among the different perceptions of literacy held by scholars, there is commonality that they "… center on the *mass media*, and on *how* and for what *purpose* messages are constructed and consumed by the masses" (Chauvin, 2003, p. 122; original emphasis). Patrick Ragains (2006) offers a useful definition of information literacy; it is "… the ability to identify, locate, and use information effectively. This definition combines critical thinking and facility with information technology" (p. 4). As Pierre Walter (1999) suggests that "... there are no simple, universal definitions of literacy, either in popular thought or scholarly theorizing" (p. 32), a variety of conceptions of literacy now exist and continue emerging in the digital age.

What becomes clear from the discussion of literacy here is that the following three points are underlying the various definitions—the ability to *analyze*, think *critically*, and create a message by oneself. Inspired by these scholars, I employ the term "critical media literacy" in this book. Through my writing, I seek to present a model of education that cultivates this new type of literacy as well as the English skills, and suggest implementing it in other higher educational institutions. John Hartley (2007) asserts the possibility of higher education in that it

> ... can be part of the push towards developing (or unleashing) creative innovation as an agent of change and growth in the knowledge-based economy; a prospect that raises these matters to the level of national policy in any country concerned with national competitiveness in a global environment. (p. 139)

Thus, colleges and universities play the significant role in guiding young minds to think and act on their own.

With the Olympic and Paralympic Games in Tokyo in 2020, MEXT offers the vision of Japanese education as follows:

> To support rapid progress toward a future that will support growth for Japan amid the accelerating globalization of the international society, it is a matter of urgency to develop the global human resources who will drive growth in Japan and be active in various

fields on the world stage, to equip them with rich language and communication skills, independence and assertiveness, and a mindset that can understand other cultures premised on in-depth understanding of Japanese culture and their own identity as Japanese. Hosting the 2020 Tokyo Olympic and Paralympic Games represents a good opportunity when the eyes of the world will turn to Japan, but it is also a critical juncture, and we need to develop the human resources who will be active on the world stage and consider matters from a global perspective. (2013b)

Hence, the English language skills and critical media literacy are essential to cope with the speed of globalization and digitalization in the present times. As already explained, this book proposes the Film-Eng praxis as a way to acquire these skills. Before illustrating an actual practice, the coming units focus on media education in Japan and Canada. Through the comparison between the two countries, I examine the ways in which literacy is promoted in the school settings and also explore the conceptual framework underneath the practice.

3
Media Education in Japan

This unit explains how media education is conceptualized and what type of literacy is promoted in Japan. Digital technology, in other words, information and communication technology (ICT) or information technology (IT) is inseparable from media education in Japan. While seeking to enhance the English language skills among students, Japan has placed emphasis on the development of ICT literacy through media education, which is called information education (*jyōhō kyōiku*). This is due to the historical background that "… Japan leads the world in the information revolution …" (Pharr, 1996, p. 4).

Acknowledging ICT skills as indispensable assets for citizens living in the 21st century, in 2001, the Japanese government founded the Strategic Headquarters for the Promotion of an Advanced Information and Telecommunications Network Society (IT Strategic Headquarters) in the Cabinet. In 2009, the IT Strategic Headquarters issued a national plan entitled *i-Japan Strategy 2015: Striving to Create a Citizen-Driven, Reassuring & Vibrant Digital Society*. This document clarifies the positive effect of digital technology on Japanese society:

> … [D]igital technology and information will lead to digital innovation and new vitality through the economy and society where individuals and society as a whole can use this vitality to undertake spontaneous and forward-looking creation and innovation … and to create a society where business enterprises will be able to shift to low-cost

and high-profit structures, sustainable economic growth and environmental and resource constraints will be balanced, and cooperation, collaboration, and coexistence with international society will be achieved. (2009, p. 2)

The IT Strategic Headquarters describe "[i]mproving and expanding the content of the information education" (2009, p. 16) as an ideal means to nurture "... highly-skilled digital human resources" (2009, p. 16), who can actualize the society as such. In this way, what becomes apparent from their plan is that the IT Strategic Headquarters regard the people's acquisition of thorough knowledge of ICT as essential for activating Japanese economy and society.

In response to this trend, MEXT articulates how to diffuse ICT knowledge and skills among the citizens in the document named *The Vision for ICT in Education: Toward the Creation of a Learning System and Schools Suitable for the 21st Century*. According to MEXT (2011), information education aims to promote:

> ... practical capability to utilize information (the ability to independently collect, judge, process, arrange, create, and express necessary information, and to transmit and convey it in accordance with the circumstances of the recipients, which also includes the ability to properly utilize information sources depending on problems and purposes) .... (p. 9)

It is obvious from here that while training students to obtain the ability described above, MEXT encourages them to turn from receivers into senders/producers of knowledge by handling ICT.

Despite the persistent promotion of ICT literacy through information education, however, the situation surrounding Japan has changed. In the document titled *Declaration to Be the World's Most Advanced IT Nation*, the IT Strategic Headquarters admit the transition: "From an international perspective, Japan has lost its status as the world's leading IT nation, and many countries have surpassed Japan in global competitiveness rankings" (2013, p. 3). In order to achieve a breakthrough and recover the position of the country, the IT Strategic Headquarters assert the importance of:

> … the digitalization of the educational environment (infrastructure including software and hardware), increasing IT literacy for all the people, bringing up the world top level of IT human resources who can take a lead in future innovation through providing opportunities (supporting environment and encouraging challenging activities to enhance individual capacity), and delivering information education with specific curriculum (curriculum prepared for specific needs and educational goals). (2013, p. 26)

The IT Strategic Headquarters point out the need to elevate ICT skills among students in the elementary, junior high, and high school levels so that all the citizens will be competent with ICT.

Media education, or rather information education in the case of Japan, which centers on the use of digital technology, enables the production of creative works and the successive generations of artists applying computer technology in the form of art. A combination of art and computer science is notable in the works of so-called digital media artists in Japan. In the article, "From the Avant-Garde: Re-Conceptualizing Cultural Origins in the Digital Media Art of Japan," Jean Ippolito (2007) focuses on three leading digital media artists since the 1980s (i.e., Masaki Fujihata, Yoichiro Kawaguchi, and Naoko Tosa), who use "… technological media —electric bells, lights, remote-control devices, etc." (p. 150). Ippolito examines how computer technology such as computer graphics and algorithm plays a key part in their artworks, and proposes the possibility that technology and art can be blended together and coexist as a piece of art.

In the case of Japan, the emphasis on digital technology results in the progression of ICT literacy through education as well as the promotion of human resources who are capable of employing technology in the form of expression. While concentrating on ICT, MEXT presents a new educational approach in order to cope with the acceleration of digitalization and globalization around the world:

> From here on, education should progress, not only through one-way teaching (i.e., lectures) or group lessons, but by utilizing ICT to adopt a new learning method that allows students to do the following: gain basic knowledge and skills through classes that match each individual's skills and specialties; learn together among other children; and identify and tackle issues by cooperating with people in their neighborhood or in foreign countries to experience various events in order to sufficiently develop a will to live, a will to learn, and intellectual curiosity. (2013a)

The statement here suggests that interactive education, to put it differently, active learning (to be discussed in detail later) is urgently needed for schools in Japan, and ICT plays a major role in advancing this new type of education. In this way, there is a new tendency to attach importance to the integration of ICT in various aspects of teaching and learning beyond the realm of information education. The next unit investigates how media education is conceptualized outside Japan by referring to Canada as an example.

4
Media Education in Canada

> TV brings the outside (with all its dangers and violence) into the peacefulness of our homes. (Marshall McLuhan, 1988a, p. 148)

This section introduces the case of media education in Ontario where Ottawa, the capital city of Canada, is situated. The Ontario Ministry of Education (OME) affirms the importance of employing ICT beyond the disciplinary boundaries. *The Ontario Curriculum, Grades 1–8: Science and Technology* enunciates: "Whenever appropriate, therefore, students should be encouraged to use ICT to support and communicate their learning" (OME, 2007a, p. 41). This statement is commonly used in other curricula such as *Technological Education* (for Grades 9–12), *Language* (for Grades 1–8), *English* (for Grades 9–12), and *The Arts* (for Grades 1–12). OME explains why the acquisition of ICT skills is promoted in education as follows:

> Students need to acquire the technological skills and knowledge that will allow them to participate fully in a competitive global economy and to become responsible citizens in an environmentally vulnerable world. To succeed in today's society, students need to be effective problem solvers and critical thinkers, able to understand, question, and respond to the implications of technological innovation.
>
> (2009a, p. 3)

While gaining ICT skills is regarded as indispensable in the subject areas indicated above, OME pronounces the necessity of cultivating "critical thinking" and "critical literacy" interdisciplinarily. For instance, *The Ontario Curriculum, Grades 1–8: The Arts* illustrates how critical literacy helps students: "Critically literate students adopt a critical stance, asking what view of the world the text advances and whether they find this view acceptable, who benefits from the text, and how the reader is influenced" (2009b, p. 53). This description is common to the Arts curricula for Grades 9–12. Moreover, *The Ontario Curriculum, Grades 9 and 10: English* gives an account of another feature:

> Critical literacy also involves asking questions and challenging the status quo, and leads students to look at issues of power and justice in society. The program empowers students by enabling them to express themselves and to speak out about issues that strongly affect them. (2007b, p. 34)

In this way, these examples show that ICT skills and critical literacy are considered to be equally important in the field of education.

Indeed, OME promotes teaching and learning "multiple literacies." These include functional literacy, numerical literacy, and media literacy besides critical literacy. In particular, OME attaches importance to cultivating media literacy of students. This is prominent in the curricula *Language* and *English*. For example, OME summarizes the content of the Language curriculum: "This curriculum organizes the knowledge and skills that students need to become literate in four strands, or broad areas of learning—Oral Communication, Reading, Writing, and Media Literacy. These areas of learning are closely interrelated ..." (2006, pp. 4–5). Accordingly, as a means to raise critical literacy and media literacy, media education has been practiced.

Scholars have pointed out the advancement of media education in Canada (see Anderson, Duncan, & Pungente, 2001; Duncan, 2005). Anderson et al. (2001) argue that the successful implementation of media education in Canadian schools is due to nationalism and the need of sustaining national identity; in Canada, there have been "... critical concerns about the pervasiveness of American popular culture ..." (p. 33). In addition, a prominent figure of media studies Marshall McLuhan has contributed to the development of media education in Canada. McLuhan suggests that "... new media—the telephone, the telegraph and radio and television" (1988b, p. 45) have changed people's daily lives and their experiences in seeing and hearing dramatically. His works on the mass media have had a great effect on the later theorization of the media. The stirring discussion of the media's role and its impact on the viewers influenced the practice of media education since 1960s and the formulation of new educational policies as well. The urgency of instructing media literacy is seen in the actions of the provincial governments of Canada, which have enacted that media education should be incorporated into school curricula (Anderson et al., 2001). Among them, Ontario is "... the first jurisdiction in North America to make media literacy a mandatory part of the curriculum, from K to Grade 12" (Duncan, 2005, p. 3).

Media literacy is defined as "[a]n informed and critical understanding of the nature of the media, the techniques used by them, and the impact of these techniques ..." and "... the ability to understand and use the mass media in an active, critical way" (OME, 2007c, p. 211). Moreover, OME presents five major concepts of media literacy as follows:

> 1. *All media are constructions.*
> 2. *The media contain beliefs and value messages.*

3. *Each person interprets messages differently.*
   4. *The media have special interests (commercial, ideological, political).*
   5. *Each medium has its own language, style, form, techniques, conventions, and aesthetics.* (2007c, p. 211)

OME acknowledges the necessity of practicing media education and promoting media literacy due to "... the power and pervasive influence these media [such as the Internet, film, and television] wield in our lives and in society" (2007b, p. 18).

Indeed, the English curriculum shows that media education plays a significant role: "Literature studies and media studies also afford both students and teachers a unique opportunity to explore the social and emotional impact of bullying, violence, and discrimination in the form of racism, sexism, or homophobia on individuals and families" (2007b, p. 34). In this way, in the case of Ontario, Canada, OME proclaims the necessity of enhancing "multiple literacies" including ICT literacy, critical literacy, and media literacy. The OME's curricula—*Science and Technology, Technological Education, Language, English,* and *The Arts*—offer clear guidelines and hints for activities in fostering these literacies, which help not only teachers develop an effective teaching plan but also students learn, step by step, to become "critical" viewers and creators as well.

5
Critical Thinking

This section illustrates the theoretical bases behind the educational policies of Japan and Canada. From the cases of media education in Japan and Ontario (Canada) have emerged some differences and similarities worth discussing. Due to their respective national agendas and positions in the globe, there are apparent differences between the two. Leaving these aside, how different and similar are they in terms of the three key points of literacy discussed earlier—the ability to analyze, think critically, and create a message by oneself? It is clear that these three are underlying education practiced in Ontario (Canada). In the case of Ontario, the model of education placing emphasis on analysis, critical thinking, and creativity reflects a combination of constructivist theory and critical pedagogy.

On the other hand, a great impact of constructivism is observable in the case of education in Japan. To be a leading nation of digital technology and innovation, Japan has been intent on promoting ICT literacy through education. With the utilization of digital media, students in information education class are encouraged to gain problem-solving skills. Japan's educational goals described earlier are consistent with the objectives of constructivist learning such as "[s]tudent knowledge creation; demonstrating student knowledge; amplifying students' voices and choices …" (Tyner, 2003, p. 383). Education under the influence of constructivist theory thus aims to help students "… express their knowledge in multiple ways, solve problems, revise their own work, and construct knowledge" (Ivers & Barron, 2006, p. 3). It is reasonable to suppose that both Japan and Ontario (Canada), acknowledging the significance of fostering the analytical and information delivery skills through education and cultivating multiple literacies including ICT literacy respectively, partly follow the model of constructivist teaching and learning, which encourages "[s]tudents and teachers [to] access, analyze, explore, and produce products using multiple media and information in a variety of ways ..." (Tyner, 2003, p. 383).

Unlike the case of Japan, however, it is obvious that the terms "critical" and "critically" are frequently used in the educational goals of Ontario (Canada). This is due to the influence of critical pedagogy proposed by Paulo Freire. Against the dominant, oppressive system sustaining the unbalanced power structure, Freire (2003) contends that "... people must first critically recognize its causes, so that through transforming action they can create a new situation ..." (p. 47). Freire thus advocates the importance of critical thinking. By this term, Freire means "... thinking which perceives reality as process, as transformation, rather than as a static entity—thinking which does not separate itself from action ..." (2003, p. 92). Here Freire asserts the necessity of accelerating critical thinking through education so that learners will turn themselves into active participants towards the just society.

Supporting Freire's argument, bell hooks (2003) claims that literacy developed in the classroom leads to critical thinking. Having recalled her response to a program interview, hooks emphasizes the significance of critical thinking as follows:

> I answered that to me "critical thinking" was the primary element allowing the possibility of change. Passionately insisting that no matter what one's class, race, gender, or social standing, I shared my

beliefs that without the capacity to think critically about our selves and our lives, none of us would be able to move forward, to change, to grow. (2003, p. 202)

In this way, hooks suggests that critical thinking is indispensable for people living in the 21st century. Moreover, Colin Lankshear and Michele Knobel (2005) elaborate on the positive function of critical thinking:

Critical thinking starts from perceiving the root causes of one's place in society—the socioeconomic, political, cultural, and historical context of our personal lives. But critical thinking continues beyond perception—toward the actions and decisions people make to shape and gain control over their lives. (p. 299)

Critical thinking is thus important, for it urges an individual to be aware of the environment around her/him, connect her/himself to the larger context, and furthermore, transform her/his thinking into action. As seen in the case of Ontario (Canada), media education influenced by critical pedagogy centers on the enhancement of critical thinking, and encourages learners to think critically about media messages and representations surrounding them. This leads to the acquisition of "critical" media literacy.

Fostering critical media literacy through education is essential in the era of accelerated digitalization and globalization. Ladislaus Semali (2000) articulates its forte:

An analysis and critique of texts and images of women, minorities, people from other cultures, ethnic groups, and images of other social groups is important to unpack, uncover, and recognize stereotypes, derogatory bias, and discrimination. Such exercise also helps to detect and understand how these texts and images help to structure our experience and identities. (p. 33)

Hence, the advancement of critical media literacy in education is crucial in order to correspond to the current phenomena that are driven visually, and it leads to making criticality practicable in the everyday life. Elevating critical media literacy in schools has the potential to inspire learners to transform themselves into producers generating alternative views in the same way as critical thinking can lead to action. Based on the argument here, the next unit shows how to apply a critical perspective in analyzing media messages and representations.

6
Decoding: Critical Analysis (Gender, Race, and Ethnicity)

A prominent figure of cultural studies Stuart Hall (1999) explored the power and impact of television on the audiences. According to Hall, between the producer and the audiences, there exists the process of "encoding" and "decoding." I looked into Hall's argument in detail elsewhere (see Hara, 2014). "Encoding" and "decoding" are important terms and key to filming. In encoding a message, a dominant meaning is produced and transmitted by the mass media involving the following five elements: "… production, circulation, distribution, consumption, reproduction" (Hall, 1999, p. 508). In consequence, the audiences conduct decoding, that is, receive and interpret the message produced by the media. Hall suggests that the viewer's interpretation is not necessarily identical with the producer's original intention. I focus on this inconsistency between the audiences and the producer later in this book. What becomes clear from Hall's critical analysis is that as viewers, we need to decode messages produced by the mass media critically. In short, it is essential to keep the following questions in mind: What kind of message is conveyed? Who creates/encodes the message? What is the intention behind the produced message? Who are the intended audiences? With these questions in mind, we can go into the habit of critical thinking.

I argue that critical thinking needs to be practiced in our daily lives since we are surrounded by various types of media. In order to understand how decoding with a critical perspective works, it is meaningful to analyze a film by Robert Flaherty, the pioneer of ethnographic film. Flaherty's *Nanook of the North* (1922) capturing the lives of the indigenous peoples in the Canadian Arctic has been a target of the debate among anthropologists. In particular, the debate over the use of narration in his film needs our attention. Some scholars admire Flaherty who invented the technique of narration using texts in ethnographic film. For instance, David MacDougall (2006) indicates:

> Flaherty's film ... proposed a narrative approach to ethnography quite unprecedented in the anthropology of the time. Like the 'life history' ethnographers published many years later, the film suggested that narrative might be one of the only ways of grasping how social forces actually converge upon an individual in society.
> (p. 233)

In his silent film shot by a 16mm camera, Flaherty used texts to tell the audiences the story of the indigenous peoples he observed and spent time with. In regards to Flaherty's use of narration, other scholars point out its problematic side. Catherine Russell (1999), for example, states:

> It is *because* of Flaherty's naturalized narrative realism, created through his 'mastery' of film language, that he could be charged with faking scenes, a charge that only authenticizes the realist context of the staging. This realism is prompted by the performances of the Inuit, as well as the drama of everyday life that they were asked to enact. (p. 110; original emphasis)

In this way, some scholars have suggested that Flaherty's use of text to narrate the indigenous lives reinforces the subjectivity of the ethnographer as the authority depicting "Reality" and the "Truth," and sustains the unequal, dichotomous relationship between the filming ethnographer and the indigenous peoples as the exotic to be filmed. Hence, "[t]he subjectivity that Flaherty creates for his characters is ... extremely limited" (Russell, 1999, p. 109).

Moreover, feminist thinkers have argued the necessity of examining the construction of femininity and masculinity and how each individual in film is gendered. For instance, Sarah Pink (2007) explains the construction of gendered identities:

> ... [H]ow both researcher and informant experience themselves and one another as gendered individuals will depend on the specific negotiation into which they enter. If visual images and technologies are part of the research project, they will play a role in how both researcher and informant identities are constructed and interpreted.
>
> (p. 26)

In the case of Flaherty's film, as the title suggests, a camera centers on the man named Nanook and his action such as building an Igloo, a snow house. Before Nanook's wife Nyla appears on the screen, a text "Nyla—The Smiling One" is presented, and the smiling woman shows up. While various outdoor activities done by Nanook are depicted, there are many shots of Nyla either holding or staying beside her baby. A feminist framework examining the construction of gendered identities urges the audiences to consider whether the division of labor portrayed in film is part of their lifestyle, or their activities are gendered and carefully constructed by the filmmaker.

Furthermore, the issue of gaze is addressed by feminist film theory (see Hara, 2014). Mary Ann Doane (1982), the pioneer of psychoanalysis on the construction and representation of femininity in cinema, shows how femininity has functioned as the pleasurable object of the male gaze.

Doane problematizes the patriarchal system that sustains the binary between male with the power to gaze and female as the gazed object. In order to deconstruct the dominant system reinforcing ideal femininity in cinema, Doane presents the concept of "female spectatorship," which enables women to have the agency to see. Applying this concept to Flaherty's film helps the audiences not only realize the power structure placing the filmmaker as the authority above the indigenous peoples— Nanook with the limited agency given by the authority and Nyla as her femininity reinforced by the filmmaker, but also pay attention to the absence, in other words, what is not depicted on the screen. Practicing "female spectatorship" means that the viewers consider what Nyla is doing outside of the frame, while Nanook is the focus of the camera. In this way, applying a critical perspective to decoding messages produced by various kinds of media makes it possible to see what is hidden, in other words, what story is untold. In addition, the utilization of a critical lens in encoding enables the producer to propose alternative perspective(s).

7
Encoding Stage 1: Employing Active Learning

As previously discussed, MEXT prioritizes cultivating English proficiency as well as ICT skills among students. In addition, nowadays, there is an urge to practice an educational method called active learning in schools in Japan. Through higher education, MEXT aims to "… develop various human resources who learn over their lifetime, think independently, and have the ability to explore and tackle issues that can deal with any situation, on the basis of a zest for life" (2013a). For this purpose, MEXT regards active learning as indispensable: "For undergraduate education, we should promote activities to change the quality of education, such as active learning (learning in which students proactively find issues and solutions), interactive lectures, practice, and experiments" (2013a). Thus, MEXT suggests that active learning is one of the core components essential for future education.

Unlike Japan, active learning has long been practiced in schools in North America. A considerable number of studies have been done to investigate the effects of active learning (e.g., Barkley, 2010; Bean, 2011; Meyers & Jones, 1993; Prince, 2004). Based on his literature review, Michael Prince (2004) indicates that the definition of active learning varies among researchers and among academic disciplines. In spite of the diverse conceptions, Prince points out the commonality: "The core elements of active learning are student activity and engagement in the learning process" (2004, p. 223).

Acknowledging the various definitions of active learning existing among literature, in this book, I consider Elizabeth Barkley's following notion useful: "Active learning means students are building their own minds through an active, involved process in which they make an idea, a concept, or a problem solution their own by assimilating it into their own understandings" (2010, p. 25). What will the classroom look like, when this kind of active learning is put into practice? Meyers and Jones (1993) delineate a drastic change:

> In an active-learning classroom, teachers no longer control students' learning by exercising power from the front of the room and depending primarily on transmitting knowledge through lectures. Instead, they direct and choreograph what happens in a classroom so that students can begin taking responsibility for their learning. (p. 56)

Active learning as such opposes the traditional teaching method originating in banking education. Freire denotes that in the banking education system, "… the students are the depositories and the teacher is the depositor. Instead of communicating, the teacher issues communiqués and makes deposits which the students patiently receive, memorize, and repeat" (2003, p. 72). Hence, active learning is necessary to reform this unbalanced relationship between teachers and students. In order to put active learning into full operation in the classroom, teachers need to be flexible and play a role as a facilitator to promote students' autonomy.

The Film-Eng praxis introduced in this book is based on active learning employed in a series of classes I taught. Here I refer to my course on media and offer a detailed account of the implementation of active learning. The objective of the course is to explore the nature of media and media representation from multiple perspectives. Students enrolled in the class focus on critical media literacy, which is essential for global communication, and examine the implications of applying it in a variety of settings such as classrooms, museums, communities, and so forth. In addition, learners investigate the social, cultural, and political relations among media producers, their subjects, and viewers. By the end of the semester, students are expected to: (1) better understand the concept of media literacy and (2) identify and analyze what and how messages are constructed by media. The course schedule is as follows:

Week 1: Introduction: New literacies for global communication
Week 2: Various forms of media in our daily lives
Week 3: Mode of address 1: Newspapers
Week 4: Mode of address 2: Television and the Internet
Week 5: Mode of response
Week 6: Representations of gender
Week 7: Representations of race and ethnicity
Week 8: The gaze and power
Week 9: Ethics in media
Week 10: Potential of media in the 21st century
Week 11: Expression through/with media for social justice
Week 12: Expression through/with media for global communication
Week 13: Presentation 1: Analysis of media representation
Week 14: Presentation 2: Application of critical media literacy
Week 15: Course review

I taught the class from September 2015 until February 2016. In this course, students completed readings assigned for each class and were engaged in activities such as discussion, group work, and presentation.

In the early phase of the course, the emphasis was on comprehending various kinds of media and the concept of media literacy. After that, students started to develop critical thinking to analyze media messages such as newspaper stories. In addition, they were encouraged to acquire critical media literacy by analyzing diverse types of media representations regarding gender, race, and ethnicity (e.g., TV commercials, music videos, and magazine advertisements). After completing analysis individually, students formed small groups and discussed their findings. Then a person from each group presented the process and the result of the discussion to class. According to John Bean (2011), this kind of activity is useful for "… promoting active learning and critical thinking … as well as accelerating students' growth as inquirers and researchers within their majors" (p. 149).

A series of discussion enabled students to build the close relationship with their classmates. This led to the emergence of the friendly atmosphere, which stimulates the active exchange of opinions and allows them to respect different values. In this way, one of the benefits of employing active learning is "… building classroom learning communities …" (Barkley, 2010, p. 27). Barkley suggests that teachers in higher education should be devoted to "… helping all students feel that they are included, honored, important, contributing members of a learning community" (2010, p. 27).

Meyers and Jones describe the consequences of establishing "a learning community" in the classroom as well as the next step essential for enhancing active learning:

> By talking and listening to one another, and by reflecting in small-group discussions, students can clarify their thinking and appreciate the perspectives of others. And once some skill in small-group participation has been mastered, students and teachers are prepared

> to move on to a more challenging form of active learning—cooperative student projects. (1993, p. 73)

After the supportive learning environment was ensured, I assigned a group project to the students enrolled in my course. The purpose of the project was to create a filming plan and present it in class. Since the number of foreign tourists visiting Japan has been increasing year after year (Naito, 2016), the students were asked to design a plan for making a TV commercial in English, which would attract more visitors to Japan. This is the initiation of the Film-Eng praxis, and it offers an example of the "cooperative student projects" discussed by Meyers and Jones. The Film-Eng praxis is inseparable from active learning illustrated in this section. At the same time, it also involves several processes, which I elucidate in the coming units.

8
Encoding Stage 2: Acquiring Film Techniques

This section presents some film techniques, which help us capture what we want with a camera. Those useful techniques include: hand-held camera, tripod use, camera movements (e.g., zoom, pan, and tilt), types of shots, angles, lighting, and sound. Learning the film techniques as such makes it possible to convey our message(s) effectively in our films.

Hand-Held Camera and Tripod Use

First, it is important to understand the following two ways of recording—hand-held filming and using a tripod. Hand-held filming means holding a camera and recording (Figure 1). If we want to capture someone or something, that is, the subject closely, the better way is doing hand-held than applying a tripod.

Figure 1. Hand-Held Filming

There are occasions that we need to make our camera as steady as possible. Attaching a camera to a tripod is helpful in that case (Figure 2). If we hold a camera in our hands and try to zoom in the subject, the image becomes very shaky. On behalf of the viewers, it is recommended to avoid such unsteady images, and putting a camera on a tripod serves our purpose.

Figure 2. Using a Tripod

Zooming

Zooming is a popular film technique, but it is important to not use it too frequently unless we have a particular reason to do so. Zooming in allows us to focus on the subject, whereas zooming out offers information of the background surrounding the subject. It is good to avoid doing too much zoom in and out. Zooming in/out quickly makes the viewers dizzy. It is useful for occasions such as filming a sports tournament. When we want the audiences to pay attention to a particular player, it is reasonable to zoom in him/her. In addition, in shooting a drama, it is effective to zoom in to show a tense atmosphere. In doing so, we can create a thrilling scene.

Panning

Panning means revolving a camera in the horizontal direction, while we are filming. It can be used effectively for showing the audiences a panoramic view or shooting a moving target. For instance, it is useful for capturing the vast expanse of the ocean or a person walking or running in the open field. It is desirable to avoid panning unless there is a reason to do so.

Figure 3. Panning the Ocean 1   Figure 4. Panning the Ocean 2

Figure 5. Panning the Ocean 3

Tilting

Tilting means revolving a camera in the vertical direction, while we are filming. This is an effectual film technique in order to show the viewers an elevated subject. For example, it is practical for capturing high buildings such as Tokyo Skytree and Tokyo Tower from the bottom to the top or the other way around. Similar to the cases of zooming and panning, it is important to do tilting, when there is a specific reason to do so.

Figure 6. Tilting a Tall Tree from Top   Figure 7. Tilting a Tall Tree to Bottom

Types of Shots

It is crucial to keep in mind the following four types of shots: wide, medium, close-up, and extreme close-up. By using a wide shot (WS), we can capture an image as wide as possible. A wide shot establishes the context of a film; it shows the audiences where the location is, who the characters are, and what is happening. Hence, it is also called an establishing shot.

Figure 8. Wide Shot

Encoding Stage 2

A medium shot (MS) offers a narrower but more detailed view compared to a wide shot. As illustrated in Figure 9, the viewers can pay close attention to the subject(s). Generally, people in a medium shot appear from above their waists.

Figure 9. Medium Shot

In a close-up shot (CS), the subject is in the center of the screen. With this shot, the audiences can grasp the details such as the reactions (e.g., disappointed, shocked, surprised, etc.) and emotions (e.g., angry, happy, sad, etc.) of the subject.

Figure 10. Close-Up Shot

An extreme close-up shot (ECS) focuses on a certain part of the subject excessively. For instance, it shows only one body part of the subject such as eye(s), mouth, hand(s), and so on. This technique is often used for advertising make-up products such as eye shadows and lipsticks.

Figure 11. Extreme Close-Up Shot of a Closed Eye

Figure 12. Extreme Close-Up Shot of an Opened Eye

In addition, there is one more called a two shot (TS), which is often applied for interviews in documentary films. It contains two people in one frame and usually focuses on an interviewee by filming over the shoulder of an interviewer.

Figure 13. Two Shot

Angles

Shooting from diverse angles adds variety and makes it possible to convey different messages. For example, by shooting from above, the subject can look vulnerable. On the other hand, shooting from below can make the subject look majestic and strong. As shown in Figure 14, filming from above allows the audiences to see a wide stretch of land. Figure 15 suggests that filming from below emphasizes the height or length of the subject.

Figure 14. Shooting from above   Figure 15. Shooting from below

I recommend filming by employing the angles and kinds of shots illustrated here. When we are shooting someone or something important, the best way is to record the same scene more than once, using these various angles and types of shots. This variety gives us many options to choose from, once we start editing on computer.

Lighting

There is a need to secure enough light and think about light sources and their effect, when shooting with a camera. It is important to not film the subject against the sun. If we do this, the subject becomes dim. It is worth understanding these two types of light—"hard" and "soft." David Pogue (2006) offers a clear definition: "Hard light comes from a small light source falling directly on an object. ... For example, when someone's standing in direct sunlight, the shadows on his face are harsh and dark" (pp. 48–9; original emphasis). Conversely, soft light is "... less direct, offering softer, smoother gradations of light from brightest to darkest areas" (Pogue, 2006, p. 49). This is also called a "diffused" light similar to "... the outdoors light on an overcast day or the light reflected from the umbrellas used by photographers" (Pogue, 2006, p. 49).

In addition, it is essential to know that filming usually involves the following three light sources—"key," "fill," and "backlight." Pogue elaborates on each light source below:

> The *key* light is the primary source of illumination in a scene. This can be the light on the camera, the sun, the overhead light above a table, or the light from a window, for example. ... The *fill* light comes from a second light source. ... It softens the shadows cast by the key light (such as the room lights). ... The *backlight* comes from behind the subject. It helps to separate the subject from the background. (2006, pp. 49–50; original emphasis)

Keeping these in mind makes a drastic change, when we do shooting.

Sound

In recording with a camera, we should not overlook the significance of sound. Gerald Millerson (2001) states that "... when you analyze most worthwhile television and film productions, you will find that for quite a lot of the time, it is the *sound* that is conveying the information and stimulating the audience's imagination ..." (p. 101; original emphasis). In this way, sound/audio plays a crucial role in filming. When we need to get clear sound/audio, it is essential to place a camera close to the subject. Using a boom microphone is desirable, but for classroom use, we can attach a microphone to the camera. Otherwise, we can record sound/audio with a voice recorder, and import it in editing software on computer during post-production. When interviewing someone, it is important to capture clear audio. However, if the recorded material is inaudible, it is possible to turn the volume up to some extent in the stage of editing (see Unit 10).

9
Encoding Stage 3: Storyboarding

A storyboard is a form on which we write down our ideas and plans in preparation for filming. Storyboarding enables us to build and elaborate our film projects. Gerald Millerson and Jim Owens (2009) offer its outline:

> The storyboard is a series of rough sketches that help the director visualize and organize his or her camera treatment. It is a visual map of how the director hopes to arrange the key shots for each scene or action sequence …. (p. 86)

By storyboarding, we provide the following important pieces of information: shot number, angle (e.g., above/below), type of shot (e.g., wide shot, medium shot, close-up shot, and extreme close-up shot), estimated time of shot, descriptions of action and dialogue, and so forth. Hence, storyboards clarify what the filmmakers intend to convey to the viewers. Conversely, we are required to make drawings of the images we have. According to Millerson and Owens, one important thing to keep in mind is that we "… don't have to be able to draw well to produce a successful storyboard" (2009, p. 87).

Storyboarding is a fundamental process before commencing filming. Millerson (2001) points out the positive effect resulting from storyboarding: "You begin to think about how one shot is going to lead into the next…. This way, you will soon get into the habit of thinking in picture sequences …" (p. 192). However, it does not mean that we need to film the scenes in order. This can be easily done, when we start editing on computer. A blank storyboard is available for classroom use (Figure 16). It has these three sections: 1) Visual, 2) Voiceover, and 3) Sound/Music. Visual columns are for sketching and showing what the film subject is/does. A voiceover means a narration and it is a place for describing what a narrator says and/or words to be shown on the screen. Sound/Music is for indicating sound effects and/or pieces of music to be used. The actual storyboard made by students in Unit 11 gives us hints in filling out the form. In any case, I recommend storyboarding and forming a plan prior to actual filming.

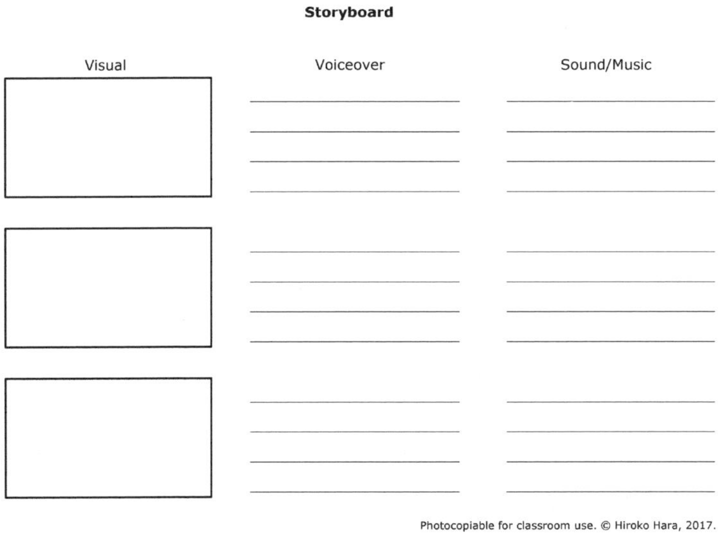

Storyboard

Visual	Voiceover	Sound/Music

Photocopiable for classroom use. © Hiroko Hara, 2017.

Figure 16. Sample Storyboard

10
Encoding Stage 4: Filming and Editing

As the last stage of encoding, I introduce filming and editing. It is time to record with a camera based on our storyboard and practice the film techniques introduced in Unit 8. Every time we do filming, it is crucial to make sure that the subject is in focus. Some film techniques such as zooming, panning, and tilting should be done not too quickly but smoothly. Hence, I recommend rehearsing camera movements before shooting. As previously discussed, it is essential to film the same scene by using various angles and types of shots. Moreover, it is important to hold our camera for at least five seconds before and after we do zooming, panning, or tilting. This gives enough space for adding transitions in the phase of editing. Before proceeding to post-production, we can play and check the footage in many ways such as playing it on the camera itself and inserting a memory card/stick into a television or a computer.

Once we are done with filming, we move to the next stage: post-production. During this phase, we edit recorded materials such as image and audio/sound by applying an editing software program. This is called non-linear editing, and what it means is that we link various recorded images and pieces of audio/sound together. This book focuses on non-linear editing with a software program "Final Cut Pro." Other popular editing software programs include "i-Movie" and "Windows Movie Maker." We can do editing by using these software programs. With "Final

Cut Pro," it is possible to: cut/trim clips such as images and pieces of audio/sound to change the duration; insert transitions to make the shift from one scene to the other smooth; adjust the volume of audio/sound; add texts on the screen; overlap several clips by changing the opacity; and many more. Since there are many books showing how to use those editing software programs available on the market, this book does not go into detail about how to use them. One thing to remember is that there are multiple ways to edit recorded data, and the one that we choose is affected by our own positionality and sense of values.

Filmmaking can be an ideal method of expression. However, there is a need to take into consideration the ethics in filming. Always make sure that we inform the subject(s) of filming in advance. It is vital to explain our intention (what we want to film and for what purpose we do recording) and ask about his/her willingness to cooperate with us. We should commence filming only if the subject agrees with his/her participation. I strongly recommend gaining his/her consent on paper. For this, we need to prepare a proper consent form, which he/she can sign. As filmmakers, we have the responsibility to answer questions, correspond to concerns, and secure his/her formal consent to participate in our film project.

Why does obtaining consent from the subject matter? The film we create represents the subject; it produces a certain representation (message) about his/her in the stage of encoding. As discussed earlier in Unit 6, it is necessary to have a critical perspective, while we are engaged in film production (both filming and editing). It is crucial to recognize that as filmmakers, we have the power to encode a particular value in our work. "The challenge," remarks Sara Kindon (2003), "… is to be more explicit about the power involved in how we work with video, to democratize its use in ways that embrace multiple and partial ways of looking and open up new possibilities for knowledge" (p. 149).

Although filmmaking makes it possible to propose alternative views verbally and visually, there is a danger that the representations we produce may lead to the (re)creation of stereotypical images and prejudices regarding the subjects. As Richard Dyer (1993) points out, "… stereotypes express particular definitions of reality, with concomitant evaluations, which in turn relate to the disposition of power within society" (p. 14). So how can filmmakers avoid (re)producing stereotypes?

In order to tackle the question as such, it is necessary for filmmakers to pay attention to the complexity, fluidity, and multiplicity of identities of the subjects. Trinh (1991) lays much emphasis on this point:

> Our experiences in life are complex, plural, and full of uncertainties. And this complexity can never be reduced and fitted into the rigid corners of ready-made solutions and filmic conventions. Mise-en-scène as the montage and recreation of the texture of life and of the inner dynamics of the subject filmed would have to incorporate the heterogeneity of living experience. (p. 112)

When we seek to reflect the diversity among people in our film production, the concept of intersectionality is useful. Lisa Loutzenheiser (2005) indicates: "Intersectionality as a concept and articulation of the complicated linkages amongst and between race, gender, class and sexuality, for example, holds great potential" (p. 27). Loutzenheiser thus suggests that the concept of intersectionality is indispensable for us living in the 21st century. Hence, it is essential for filmmakers to acknowledge the multi-layered elements (re)constructing the identity of the subject and avoid placing him/her into a simple, single category.

11
Film-Eng Praxis in Practice

This unit describes the initiation and development of the group project introduced in Unit 7. To be successful in the Film-Eng praxis, there are several processes, which students have to go through. These include: acquiring the critical thinking skills and the film techniques, learning how to do storyboarding, filming, and editing, and finally, producing a certain visual expression using English. The Film-Eng praxis implemented in my class is under the influence of Freire's statement below:

> For apart from inquiry, apart from the praxis, individuals cannot be truly human. Knowledge emerges only through invention and re-invention, through the restless, impatient, continuing, hopeful inquiry human beings pursue in the world, with the world, and with each other. (2003, p. 72)

Freire thus contends that both inquiry and praxis are essential components of education. This section shows how the Film-Eng praxis cultivates these two important elements, thereby illustrating how it can make the teaching and learning environment lively.

Launching Praxis

As already discussed in Unit 7, the purpose of the group project is to design a TV commercial to attract foreign visitors to Japan, and do a presentation about it. The number of students enrolled in the class was 31, and they formed groups of 2 to 5 members voluntarily (Figure 17).

Arts-Based Education to Become Global Citizens

Figure 17. Students Forming Groups

It turned out that the groups were the same as the ones that held a series of discussions. This is highly productive because discussing various topics with the same members every week can "... promote student interaction and friendships, help students develop leadership skills, and foster diversity" (Bean, 2011, p. 201). In the groups formed for the Film-Eng praxis, the students exchanged their contact information by using one of the most popular social networking services (SNS) among them so that they could get in touch with each other easily. In addition, each group appointed a project manager to facilitate the group members, and came up with a production company name for their TV commercial.

Developing Praxis

Through lectures and discussions, the learners gained knowledge of media; for example, the relationship between encoding and decoding, and diverse messages produced and distributed by various kinds of media around the world. Unlike decoding as receivers of media messages, the Film-Eng praxis allows the students to do encoding, in other words, become senders of messages by creating a TV commercial plan on their own. The targeted audiences of their commercial are people in other countries, and the principal message to encode is: "Go on a trip and explore

Japan." Each group received a storyboard form to fill in. All the students in the class were new to storyboarding, so I explained its purpose and what to include, and emphasized the importance of drawing images and elaborating on voiceover/narration as well as sound/music (refer to Unit 9 for storyboarding). In particular, in preparation to draw images, I held a camera workshop to teach the film techniques such as camera movements, types of shots, angles, and so forth (see Unit 8). This helped them discuss and decide what would be appropriate for each shot while storyboarding.

With all these skills and knowledge obtained, I offered the following questions to consider for all the groups:

> Story: What story do you want to tell the viewers?
> Characters: Who and/or what will appear in your commercial?
> Narration: Do you use someone's voice or put text on the screen as a narration?
> Music/Sound: What kind of music/sound is good and effective?

Each group did brainstorming and exchanged their opinions based on the questions above (Figure 18). After active discussions, they put their thoughts together and came up with a theme for their commercial.

Figure 18. Students Discussing Ideas

Arts-Based Education to Become Global Citizens

Storyboarding

After their respective themes were fixed, all the groups began storyboarding. First, they started making a drawing of each shot in sequence (Figure 19).

Figure 19. Storyboarding

The students thought about the order of shots carefully and communicated with their group members about the camera work, narration, and music/sound appropriate for each shot (Figure 20).

Figure 20. Students Discussing their Storyboard

Many groups used color pens and pencils for their respective storyboards so that the audiences could have a better understanding of the commercial

52

on a presentation day (Figure 21).

Figure 21. Students Coloring their Storyboard

Some students found difficulty in creating a narration in English, so I checked each group and helped them translate what they wanted to say from Japanese into English. Prior to their presentations, I proofread and confirmed the narrative parts with all the groups, and their storyboards were finally completed (see Figures 22 and 23 as examples).

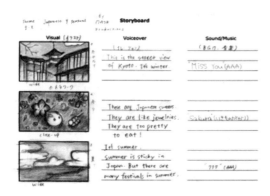

Figure 22. Completed Storyboard (Page 1)

Arts-Based Education to Become Global Citizens

Figure 23. Completed Storyboard (Page 2)

Presentation

In preparation for their presentation, each group decided who was presenting which part, and those who were in charge of reading an English narration aloud practiced pronunciation with me. A total of 10 groups presented their storyboards. To make it easier for the audiences to see the completed storyboard, each group used an overhead projector (OHP) connected to the digital projection system (Figure 24).

Figure 24. Presenting with the Digital Projection System

While playing music/sound with their smartphone, each group showed a series of images of shots and read the narration aloud. Then they explained their storyboard based on the questions discussed earlier. They also talked about the theme and indicated why they made specific decisions in terms of the story, character(s), narration, and music/sound (Figure 25). The themes they created include: "Famous Places in Japan," "Japanese Food," "Japanese Four Seasons," "Japanese Flowers," "Short Trip," "Japanese *Kawaii*," "5 Rangers and Images of Japan," and so on.

Figure 25. Students Presenting their Storyboard

When a group was presenting, the audiences were well-mannered (Figure 26); they were intent on the presentations of other groups and applauded the presenters. In this way, it is essential for the instructor to create this kind of space where students listen to each other in the respectful manner.

Figure 26. Presenters and Viewers

Outcomes of Praxis

This section summarizes the outcomes of the Film-Eng Praxis. Taking account of the characteristics and the guidelines of "interactive" research methods described by Ted Palys (2003), I conducted a questionnaire survey on February 1, 2016. I asked the students both structured questions and open-ended questions (Table 1) in order to focus on their voices and examine how they felt about being engaged in the praxis.

Table 1. Sample Questionnaire Questions

Structured questions:
How was the group project? (Circle one)
- 5 Great
- 4 Good
- 3 OK
- 2 Not so good
- 1 Bad

Do you hope to make a movie based on the storyboard, if this is a one-year class? (Circle one)
- 5 Definitely want to do so
- 4 Want to do so
- 3 Feel like doing so
- 2 Not so much
- 1 Not at all

Open-ended questions:
What do you think about the film techniques you learned?
What do you think about storyboarding?
What did you learn from the group project?

First of all, the responses from the students suggest that the camera workshop in which I taught the film techniques such as camera movements, types of shots, and angles was useful:

> K: I started to look at scenes in TV commercials and dramas based on the way of the camera work.
> H: I want to refer to these film techniques when I take pictures.
> Y.I: I want to make a movie, using the film techniques I learned.

It is reasonable to suppose here that teaching the film techniques lets some students have a refreshing view on the mass media and apply what they have learned in class to their daily lives.

In terms of storyboarding launched after the camera workshop, many students have comments similar to Hase and Gracia's:

> Hase: This was my first time to make a storyboard, so it was a good experience.
> Gracia: We had to draw pictures and think about music by ourselves, so it was very hard but fun.

It becomes clear from their words above that enjoyment and hardship are intermingled in the students' feelings. The same kind of situation can be found in what M.K remarks regarding presenting a storyboard: "I felt it was difficult to convey to the listeners what we wanted to say, and also it was enjoyable to make one thing together with the members."

The survey results indicate that while facing difficulties, many students favor the group presentation session and they have learned a variety of things:

> Marie: It was pleasant to express to the audiences what our group

wanted to tell within the limited space and time.

RV: I was able to learn the procedures and how to proceed with a presentation.

Wakii: Each group pronounced English well. It was easy to see their storyboards because they were good at drawing.

Indeed, a great number of students relish working on the group project. This is clearly shown in their following responses.

Table 2. Students' Views on the Group Project

How was the group project? (Circle one)	n	%
5 Great	22	70.97
4 Good	7	22.58
3 OK	2	6.45
2 Not so good		
1 Bad		
Total	31	100.00

As seen in Table 2, approximately 71% of the students gave the highest rating to their experiences of working in a group.

Many students answered that they learned the importance of cooperation through the group project. Chyon's statement: "I found it was delightful to think and act in cooperation with the members!" represents the majority opinion in favor of group work. However, cooperation is not always easy, as Jacky's words suggest: "I realized the difficulty as well as the fun of being at work, consulting with my friends." On the other hand, some students can obtain a rich learning experience after overcoming the difficulties. As Spring points out: "I learned the importance of working together and supplementing each person's weak point," cooperative learning can raise the student's consciousness as an active learner.

In order to actualize cooperative learning, which has positive consequences such as this, Barkley (2010) enunciates:

> Becoming a true learning community is hard work. It requires students to move beyond comfortable passivity and take risks, assume new roles, and develop skills that are different from those they are accustomed to using in many college classrooms. It requires students to work together and resolve conflicts in ways that acknowledge divergence of opinion and respect individual differences. (pp. 125–6)

Applying what Barkley mentions here to the case of the Film-Eng Praxis, we can say that "a true learning community" emerges when the students dare to get out of the comfort zone and start expressing themselves and listening to others in the positive, welcoming space facilitated by the instructor. This is supported by Minzy's response: "Creating something together not by insisting on our own opinions but by exchanging our views made our product better compared to what I imagined."

Moreover, the survey results reveal another interesting point about the Film-Eng Praxis below.

Table 3. Students' Views on Making a Movie

Do you hope to make a movie based on the storyboard, if this is a one-year class? (Circle one)	n	%
5 Definitely want to do so	9	29.03
4 Want to do so	14	45.16
3 Feel like doing so	7	22.58
2 Not so much		
1 Not at all	1	3.23
Total	31	100.00

What becomes obvious from the responses of the students is that many of them have a forward-looking attitude towards producing a movie based on what was covered in the course. This is a one-semester class running from September until February, in other words, we are limited in time and completing a storyboard as a visual expression is the best we can do. If this is a one-year class, it is possible to do filming based on the finished storyboard. From April to August, students learn all the materials illustrated in Units 6 to 10, and from September to February, they carry out filming and editing, and screen their movies in the end. The questionnaire survey discloses that a large number of students are favorable to the Film-Eng Praxis. Thus, I recommend instructors to have flexibility and implement the praxis appropriate for the objectives, size, duration, and student body of each class. The next unit introduces a product of the Film-Eng Praxis.

12
Film Script

Yugen
4–minute digital video
Produced by Hiroko Hara in collaboration with Hara Pekkori Girls Productions
Edited by Hiroko Hara
Year of Release: 2015
Filming Location: Japan
Voices: Samantha as Voice 1, Jasmine as Voice 2, Canaco as Voice 3, and Lisa as Voice 4
Music: "Beyond Consonance and Dissonance" by Hiroko Hara
Rhythm: Canaco, Jasmine, Lisa, and Samantha

Voice 1: West/East
Voice 2: Here/There
Voice 3: Center/Margin
Voice 4: Origin/Destination

Figure 27. Still 1 from *Yugen*. 4–minute digital video. 2015.
© Hiroko Hara, 2015.

Voice 1:
West/East
Japanese/Non-Japanese
Simplicity/Complexity

Text on screen:
Sui-sui
Smooth

Hira-hira
Fluttering

Voice 2:
Here/There
Now/Then
Body/Soul

Text on screen:
Puka-puka
Floating

Sara-sara
Rustling

Voice 3:
Light/Darkness
Center/Margin
Old/New

Text on screen:
Pika-pika
Sparkling

Yura-yura
Wavering

Voice 4:
Insider/Outsider
Visible/Invisible
Origin/Destination

Text on screen:
Huwa-huwa
Airy

Iki-iki
Full of life

Figure 28. Still 2 from *Yugen*. 4–minute digital video. 2015.
© Hiroko Hara, 2015.

Voice 1:
West and East blurred
Japanese and non-Japanese blurred
Simplicity and complexity blurred

Voice 2:
Here and there blurred

Now and then blurred
Body and soul blurred

Voice 3:
Light and darkness blurred
Center and margin blurred
Old and new blurred

Voice 4:
Insider and outsider blurred
Visible and invisible blurred
Origin and destination blurred

Figure 29. Still 3 from *Yugen*. 4–minute digital video. 2015.
© Hiroko Hara, 2015.

Voice 1:
West/East
Japanese/Non-Japanese
Simplicity/Complexity

Text on screen:
Sui-sui
Smooth

Film Script

Hira-hira
Fluttering

Voice 2:
Here/There
Now/Then
Body/Soul

Text on screen:
Puka-puka
Floating

Sara-sara
Rustling

Voice 3:
Light/Darkness
Center/Margin
Old/New

Text on screen:
Pika-pika
Sparkling

Yura-yura
Wavering

Voice 4:
Insider/Outsider
Visible/Invisible
Origin/Destination
(Voices 1–4 in layers)

Text on screen:
Huwa-huwa
Airy

Iki-iki
Full of life

Figure 30. Still 4 from *Yugen*. 4–minute digital video. 2015.
© Hiroko Hara, 2015.

Voice 1:
West and East blurred
Japanese and non-Japanese blurred
Simplicity and complexity blurred

                                                Voice 2:
                                                Here and there blurred
                                                Now and then blurred
                                                Body and soul blurred

Voice 3:
Light and darkness blurred
Center and margin blurred
Old and new blurred

Film Script

Voice 4:

Insider and outsider blurred
Visible and invisible blurred
Origin and destination blurred
(Voices 1–4 in layers)

Text on screen:
With a brush in your hand,
what will you express?

Figure 31. Still 5 from *Yugen*. 4–minute digital video. 2015.
© Hiroko Hara, 2015.

Now it is your turn.

13

Case Study of the Film Project

> Again, in a role of graceful and subtle elegance, you should not forget the principle of strength. (Zeami, 2006, p. 119)

The previous unit presented the script of a film entitled *Yugen* (2015) with some still images excerpted from it. It was filmed and produced in collaboration with my second-year seminar students in 2015. Although the seminar is small-scale, it is year-round, so the students have enough time to practice the Film-Eng Praxis and complete a film. Therefore, this particular praxis can offer a model useful for both small and large classes running throughout the year. In addition, their film serves as a good example showing how students in higher education can express their views verbally and visually, after having gained the skills of decoding and encoding as well as the film techniques. There are four major points, which compose the conceptual framework of the film: the concept of *yugen*, calligraphy, storytelling, and rhythm. This unit gives a full account of each point.

Concept of *Yugen*

All the members of my seminar—Canaco, Jasmine, Lisa, and Samantha—have experience of studying abroad such as in the United States of America and Australia, and they were asked questions about Japanese culture by local people in common. Therefore, they did some research on concepts rooted in Japanese culture and through active discussions, they reached the conclusion that applying the concept of *yugen* was appropriate for their film project. It is said that a Noh master Zeami expanded the concept of *yugen* through his theory and practice of Noh plays. William Wilson, the translator of Zeami's *Fushikaden*, elaborates on the concept of *yugen* as follows:

> In early Japanese poetic aesthetics, it meant the deep and unknowable, yet elegant in the pathos of things. Later, it began to mean a graceful and subtle beauty, and an elegant simplicity and gentleness with a touch of melancholy. Zeami inherited and was familiar with all of these meanings and nuances. (2006, p. 170)

The seminar members agreed that some delicate and profound features are embraced in Japanese culture, and that the concept of *yugen* is ideal for visualizing those since it holds "… the ability to imply, rather than to expose something in its entirety; to suggest and evoke, rather than to delineate laboriously" (Trinh, 1991, p. 162).

Calligraphy (*Shodo*)

The film production team paid attention to the significance of calligraphy (*shodo*). Calligraphy is one of the key cultural practices, as Samantha says, "We learn calligraphy in schools in Japan from the early age." Drawing on the concept of *yugen* described above, they decided to practice ink painting (*suibokuga*) in their film. Jasmine explains the reason: "Calligraphy is a Japanese tradition. I want to tell people that it is possible to not only write a word but draw a picture by using a brush."

The concept of *yugen* has a great effect on ink painting, as Naomi Okamoto (2015) points out: "Japanese ink painting combines the traditional aesthetic of simplicity with a distinct emphasis on intuitive expression"

(p. 8). With regard to ink painting, it is important to give consideration to the color of ink. According to Yolanda Mayhall (1989), "A composition can emerge in black, shades of gray, and white ... that can suggest a whole spectrum of color" (p. 9). In addition, Canaco, who created an ink painting of a wolf in the film, remarks: "I drew a wolf with a brush. It is splendid about Japanese culture that we can express what we want by the light and shade of one color." The potential of the gray color in ink painting is proclaimed by Trinh: "The new hue is a distinct color of its own, neither black nor white but somewhere midway, where possibilities are indefinite" (2013, p. 125).

Moreover, handwriting with a brush is not a mere literal expression. "The brush," mentions William Reed (1989), "magnifies the power of concepts which are difficult to put into words. The act of painting itself is intense and immediate, but it leaves a lasting trace, a vivid impression of the mind that produced it" (p. 23). In this way, by drawing a picture with a brush and through the color emerging from a combination of a brush, ink, and paper, the film production team intended to embody the concept of *yugen* and provoke a new set of images and feelings among the viewers.

Storytelling

Generally, a film has a narrator, who tells a story to the audiences. In her work *D-Passage: The Digital Way*, Trinh (2013) focuses on storytelling in a film and suggests that it is important for a filmmaker to consider how she/he positions her/himself, how she/he should tell stories, and what and whose stories she/he should tell. The film production team decided to tell stories from the position influenced by the notion of the gray color, and aimed to inspire a new view transgressing binary oppositions such as black and white. For this purpose, the film *Yugen* has four storytellers, who vocalize English antonyms such as origin/destination, here/there, insider/outsider, now/then, and so forth (see Unit 12).

The experience of having studied abroad exerts a great influence on the seminar members. For instance, Jasmine talks about the transformation of the self through her study in the United States:

> When I was a first-year college student, I went to a foreign country for the first time in my life! I found it was very difficult to learn the language other than my mother tongue. But I came to be able to have more smooth communication in English than before, and realized my growth as a person.

Looking back on her experience in the United States, Lisa says, "I think the words like here/there, origin/destination, and insider/outsider represent encounters and connections with people from various countries while studying abroad." As her words show, the storytellers of the film *Yugen* refer to blending the binary elements such as "here and there blurred," "origin and destination blurred," "insider/outsider blurred," and "West and East blurred." In this way, they recorded their voices reading aloud the words that are closely related to their experience.

In addition to English, the film production team decided to explore the language they grew up with. A great figure of postcolonial studies Ngũgĩ wa Thiong'o (1986) articulates the mutual relationship between language and culture:

> Language carries culture, and culture carries, particularly through orature and literature, the entire body of values by which we come to perceive ourselves and our place in the world. How people perceive themselves affects how they look at their culture, at their politics and at the social production of wealth, at their entire relationship to

nature and to other beings. Language is thus inseparable from ourselves as a community of human beings with a specific form and character, a specific history, a specific relationship to the world.

(p. 16)

Taking Ngũgĩ's words into consideration, the seminar members chose to use both Japanese and English—the first and the second languages for them—as a method of storytelling.

After that, the film production team discussed striking points of the Japanese language and realized the fact that it has plenty of onomatopoeic words. According to Hiroko Fukuda (2003), onomatopoeia is rooted in Japanese culture:

> This is no small thing, for onomatopoeia is one of the most fundamental, characteristic, and lively aspects of the Japanese language. For native Japanese speakers, onomatopoeia are not just words; they are windows through which they view the world. These words represent, to a considerable extent, the Japanese perception of life.
>
> (p. 9)

Indeed, onomatopoeia is close to the daily lives of the seminar members, as seen in Canaco's statement: "We often use onomatopoeia in school." Focusing on onomatopoeia, Susan Millington (1993) indicates how Japanese differs from English: "In general, their language is rich in words expressing feeling; English in words of action" (p. 12). Millington explains a distinguishing characteristic of the Japanese language in that "… the Japanese are extremely sensitive to how things feel, and there are many onomatopoeic phrases to describe the touch or feel of something …" (1993, p. 12). As Samantha says, "I want people to know about a variety of onomatopoeia," the production team came up with the following onomatopoeic terms—smooth (*sui-sui*), fluttering (*hira-hira*), floating (*puka-puka*), rustling (*sara-sara*), sparkling (*pika-pika*), wavering (*yura-yura*), airy (*huwa-huwa*), and full of life (*iki-iki*)—and put them in the film.

Rhythm

In addition to storytelling, Trinh (1999) suggests that rhythm plays a key role in films: "Whether one is conscious of it or not, rhythm marks one's experience of film and allows one to remember it, even if one cannot articulate it in the immediate present" (p. 198). The production team attached importance to the creation of rhythm for their film. They made a beat and tapped out rhythm by using plastic cups. After a lot of practice, they recorded their performance (see Figure 32).

Figure 32. Seminar Members Creating Rhythm

In accordance with the rhythm they created, I composed a piece of music entitled "Beyond Consonance and Dissonance," which is a fast tempo and completes itself with the performance of the rhythm.

In addition, it is worth paying attention to the rhythm embraced in languages. The following seminar members point out the rhythm and the sound of English. "Having studied abroad," remarks Lisa, "I felt communication in English more familiar to me, and found it enjoyable to vocalize and pronounce, so I wanted to show this enjoyment along with music."

Moreover, Jasmine says, "I was careful about my pronunciation of English. I have difficulty differentiating the pronunciation of consonants like r/l and b/v, in which Japanese people are weak."

In this way, Canaco, Jasmine, Lisa, and Samantha formed the conceptual framework underlying the film *Yugen*, and did recording. In this film project, I played a role as a composer, editor, and producer; I consulted with them about my editing and asked them what to keep and delete. After the consultation, the film was completed and screened at a school festival in October 2015. In the group interview, all the team members recommended practicing the Film-Eng praxis.

> Canaco: Using English allowed me to reconsider Japanese culture conversely. I recommend using English and making a film to college students.

> Samantha: Yes, I do. It is because there are things that can be expressed only in English.

> Lisa: I highly recommend it! We were able to create a film with an original message by combining music, language, and Japanese culture.

> Jasmine: I had a lot of fun in creating a work together with friends, who were fond of English. It was also wonderful that we created the rhythm by ourselves.

Thus, the film production team is proud of the film *Yugen*. The members and I now seek to submit the work to film festivals in and outside Japan.

14

Audience

> By necessity, our Way is an art that makes the viewer its very foundation .... (Zeami, 2006, pp. 104–5)

As explained previously, Hall (1999) explored the intricate relationship between encoding and decoding in the mass media (see Unit 6). Elizabeth Ellsworth (1997) investigates it from a perspective of film studies as well as educational studies, and calls the former "address" and the latter "response." According to Ellsworth, the act of the filmmaker conveying certain messages/information to the targeted audiences is a "mode of address," while what the audience takes from a film is a "mode of response."

Ellsworth's argument can be applied to the film *Yugen*, for it has both modes of address and response. "Different formal and stylistic systems in a single film," remarks Ellsworth, "can have different modes of address. Multiple modes of address can be going on simultaneously" (1997, p. 27). Indeed, *Yugen* has more than one mode of address since there are several messages that the production team members hope to convey. These include the profundity of ink painting, the abundance of Japanese onomatopoeic expressions, and the enjoyment involved with communicating in English.

As Ellsworth indicates: "Films have intended and imagined audiences. They also have desired audiences" (1997, p. 23), the production team set up the targeted audiences in developing the film project. Using both

Japanese and English in the film, they intend to convey the messages discussed above to college students, who have been learning English and/or have experience studying abroad, and also to people living outside Japan. Telling stories from the "gray" position, the film production team hope to invite multiple ways of interpretation among the viewers. Trinh (1991) explains what should be done to achieve this:

> To bring out the plural, sliding relationship between ear and eye and to leave more room for the spectators to decide what they want to make out of a statement or a sequence of images, it is necessary to invent a whole range of strategies that would unsettle such fixedness.
> (p. 206)

What she/he gains by studying abroad and the way of leading a school life in Japan vary among students. Therefore, the production team avoids forcing a single, fixed view, and encourages the viewers to reflect on their own experience and lifestyle through the film *Yugen*.

Then how do the intended viewers interpret the film? Does their mode of response match with the filmmakers' intention? In order to examine these questions, it is crucial to consult with students, who fulfill the conditions as the targeted audiences, and inquire how they interpret the film. All the students in my first-year seminar in 2015—Charlotte, Jessica, Karen, Lily, and Noelu—have experience studying abroad in the United States. They read an English textbook on media studies and acquired critical media literacy illustrated in Unit 5. As a seminar activity, they watched and discussed the film *Yugen*. The discussion started with the first impression of the film.

> Noelu: I don't understand it. What's the meaning of *suibokuga*? What's the meaning of *yugen*?

> Karen: It's too difficult for me. I want to watch the movie again.
>
> Lily: I can't understand why they use opposite words. It's difficult for me.
>
> Charlotte: At first, I thought the film was about language because there were many words in it. But there were scenes of drawing a picture in the middle. I don't understand what the film tries to tell us.
>
> Jessica: It's difficult for me, so I want to watch it again.

As suggested by Karen and Jessica, they watched the film once again and concentrated their attention to apprehend it.

Due to the multiple modes of address contained in *Yugen*, the five students focused on diverse elements of the film. Jessica and Noelu stated that ink painting was the most remarkable, while the way of vocalizing English antonyms was the most impressive to Karen. Charlotte and Lily remarked that the use of the word "blurred" was the most striking.

In addition to these impressions, they had various questions regarding the film.

> Jessica: What's the purpose of showing onomatopoeia on the screen?
>
> Lily: Why did they choose onomatopoeia, opposite words, and *suibokuga*?
>
> Noelu: Why did they draw pictures?
>
> Charlotte: Why do antonyms and onomatopoeia appear in the film?

> Karen: When someone says something, another person speaks, too. Their voices overlap. What's the reason for this?

Raising the questions above, they also discussed what was difficult and confusing about the film. It was common that everyone had difficulty comprehending the relation among the image, the text, and the voice in the film. They see the performance of ink panting and the Japanese onomatopoeic words on the screen, while they hear the storytellers pronouncing the antonyms in English. In addition, the way in which the antonyms are vocalized changes towards the ending of the film. In the beginning, each storyteller reads the words aloud respectively. Then their voices overlap with each other, and there emerges a layer of voices. The film repeats this process, which results in confusing the viewers. Trinh's following analysis is helpful in this case: "Cutting a sentence at different places, for example, assembling it with holes, repeating it in slightly different forms and in ever-changing verbal and visual contexts help to produce a constant shift and dislocation in meanings" (1991, p. 206). It is reasonable to suppose that the film *Yugen* has the function as such.

Difficulty and confusion reported by the viewers are natural reactions. Ellsworth elaborates on the address-and-response relationship between the filmmaker and the audiences:

> No matter how much the film's mode of address tries to construct a fixed and coherent position within knowledge, gender, race, sexuality, from which the film "should" be read; actual viewers have always read films against their modes of address, and "answered" films from places different from the ones that the film speaks to.
> (1997, p. 31; original emphasis)

Ellsworth thus points out that the filmmaker's mode(s) of address and the response(s) of the audiences do not necessarily match together. Similarly, focusing on how students view classroom videos, Kevin Miller and Xiaobin Zhou (2007) denote that "… viewers bring a variety of different kinds of filters …" (p. 332). According to Ellsworth, disagreement/inconsistency should not be removed. Indeed, tension is inevitable for the creation of not the one-sided but the interactive relationship between the filmmaker and the audiences. Trinh (1991) regards this reciprocity as "mutual learning," and suggests that "… the relation between filmmaker, filmed subject, and film viewer becomes so tightly interdependent that the reading of the film can never be reduced to the filmmaker's intentions" (p. 109).

As Trinh indicates, various ways of reading the film *Yugen* are possible. It is clearly shown in the comments of the five students below.

> Karen: In the film, there are onomatopoeic words peculiar to Japan. Similarly, there are many things unique to America. For example, there are special events like Thanksgiving Day. I experienced them for the first time, when I was studying there.

> Charlotte: Besides writing characters and drawing pictures, there is a way of expressing the self without words in Japan. The movie made me think about nonverbal communications like sensing how other people may feel. On the other hand, in America, I noticed the most important thing was to utter opinions.

> Jessica: This movie has many opposite words. I think joining two things that oppose each other creates something new.

> Noelu: This movie reminds me of my student life in California. There I was able to take off my bias and widen my perspective by communicating with people from various countries. To stop

biases, it is important to put oneself in the place where cultures contact each other.

Lily: The message I got from the movie was that we need to rethink the view creating the opposite and think wholly.

In this way, it is obvious that each student interpreted the film differently. Trinh refers to a film that promotes fertile imaginations without compelling a fixed message:

> Reading a film is a creative act and I will continue to make films whose reading I may provoke and initiate but do not control. A film is like a page of paper which I offer the viewers. I am responsible for what is within the boundary of the paper but I do not control and do not wish to control its folding. The viewers can fold it horizontally, obliquely, vertically; they can weave the elements to their liking and background. This interfolding and interviewing situation is what I consider to be most exciting in making films. (1991, p. 109)

Thus, it is essential for the filmmaker to direct her/his attention to the intricate relationship between the film producer and the audiences, and acknowledge diverse ways of reaction and interpretation by the viewers.

15
Conclusion

For me, self-expression through art and self-expression through writing are essentially the same thing. Both offer methods of discovering new territories of the mind. And with both, I always aim to be in the vanguard. (Kusama, 2011, p. 206)

We can no longer disregard the impact of visual culture and technology on our daily lives. The practice of teaching and learning is inseparable from the current trend of taking pictures, recording videos, and sharing them through social networking services. Hence, educational practice needs to evolve itself so that the young generation can participate actively in the globalizing and digitalized world. For this, I have suggested that the arts play a crucial role in encouraging young minds to become eager learners and thereby grow into vigorous citizens.

Researchers have pointed out the positive aspects of integrating the arts into the realm of education (e.g., Goldberg, 2001; Goodlad & Morrison, 1980; Shohat & Stam, 1994). For instance, John Goodlad and Jack Morrison (1980) describe its advantage as follows:

> The pedagogical beauty of the arts, properly conceived and taught, is that they offer unlimited self-involvement on the part of the learner. … [E]xperiences leading to new ones and the evolving interpretation of these experiences provide ends and means simultaneously. (p. 11)

Goodlad and Morrison thus indicate that employing the arts in education produces a good effect on learners.

Merryl Goldberg (2001) also elucidates the power of the arts leading to a positive change in the context of schooling:

> The arts serve as a methodology or strategy for learning—expanding traditional teaching methods into a fascinating and imaginative forum for exploration of subject matter. Using the arts as a teaching tool in the classroom broadens their function from the more traditional model of teaching *about* the arts and provides opportunities for students to transform understanding and apply their ideas in a creative form. (p. 25; original emphasis)

Here Goldberg pronounces that alternative modes of teaching and learning emerge from the application of the arts in the curriculum. In addition, Goldberg contends that putting the arts to practical use in the educational settings makes diverse ways of expressing opinions and dealing with knowledge construction possible: "As a language of expression, art gives rise to many voices in the classroom and opens many avenues for all students to work with knowledge" (2001, p. 25).

In this trend, scholars have attested that arts-based education and research embrace many possibilities (e.g., Barone & Eisner, 2012; Eisner, 2002; Hickman, 2007; Leavy, 2015; Siegesmund & Cahnmann-Taylor, 2008). Richard Siegesmund and Melisa Cahnmann-Taylor (2008), for example, portray the potential of utilizing the arts in schooling as well as educational research:

> Arts-based educational research is particularly well suited for understanding—and demystifying—the human relationships that enhance learning. Such research can provide evidence that helps us under-

stand how excellent teaching engages students in the structures of deep learning. The outcome of such learning is personal agency: autonomous individuals who have the capacity to imaginatively shape their own lives by having the courage to write their own stories. (p. 244)

In this way, Siegesmund and Cahnmann-Taylor proclaim that artistic inquiry and practice function as the powerful instrument not only for enriching the quality of learning but also for fostering students' autonomy in expression and creation.

The Film-Eng praxis introduced in this book entails the positive features as such. As I discussed elsewhere (see Hara, 2016), filmmaking serves as a good example of arts-based approaches in education. Incorporating video/film production in education and research destabilizes the border between the written text and the visual image, and helps researchers/educators and learners yield new views resisting and challenging essentialization, categorization, and dichotomization. In addition, in the case of the Film-Eng praxis, it helps learners enhance their English language skills as well as critical media literacy. Paying attention to the spread of the English language as a *lingua franca* around the globe, Braj Kachru (2006) states that "… contemporary English does not have just one defining context but many—across cultures and languages" (p. 275). In the situation as such, there is a need to promote diverse styles of expression using English. Ryuko Kubota (2004) asserts the necessity of practicing "critical multicultural education" and for both teachers and students:

> It is necessary to acknowledge that assimilation into the Eurocentric norm often underlies the superficial celebration of diversity preventing the diversification of worldviews and linguistic forms. In order

to affirm genuine pluralism and multiplicity, it is necessary to interrogate existing power relations that sustain a hierarchy of multiple perspectives and linguistic forms and to explore possibilities for oppositional discourses. (pp. 45–6)

The Film-Eng praxis makes a contribution to the emergence of veritable diversity discussed here.

As illustrated earlier, fostering critical media literacy is indispensable for succeeding in the implementation of video/film production in class. According to Allan Luke (2014), this new type of literacy is required in order to "… analyze, critique, and transform the norms, rule systems, and practices governing the social fields of institutions and everyday life …" (p. 21). Hence, acquiring critical media literacy enables students to become active global citizens with the advanced abilities of decoding various messages and encoding alternative ideas, who can contribute to the realization of the more just world.

Moreover, the Film-Eng praxis accelerates critical thinking and active learning, which are both necessary for the young generation to create their own future in the 21st century. Ella Shohat and Robert Stam (1994) indicate the great efficacy of applying audio and visual materials to teaching. They call it "… audio-visual pedagogy" (1994, p. 10) and suggest what this pedagogy does is to "… deploy the social heteroglossia of the classroom itself to call attention to the students' own ideological assumptions and affective investments" (1994, p. 357). Utilizing the audio and the visual in education elevates students' critical thinking, which leads to the awareness and affirmation of diversity in terms of nationality, race, ethnicity, gender, and so forth. Hence, the cultivation of critical thinking in education is essential since it helps learners recognize the environment around them, connect themselves to the larger context, and furthermore, transform thinking into action.

In addition, active learning urges both teachers and students to move beyond the conventional way of teaching and learning, which originated in banking education. To put this new educational approach into practice in class, both sides have to make all possible efforts. Instructors are required to have flexibility, play a role as facilitators, and create a positive, encouraging atmosphere in the classroom in order to promote students' autonomy. Learners need to step out of the comfort zone and listen to different values, while voicing their opinions. Both educators and students have an obligation to cultivate this cooperative, tolerant space in which diversity is acknowledged. When the efforts of teachers and those of learners overlap each other, "a true learning community" (Barkley, 2010, p. 125) comes into being. Meyers and Jones (1993) summarize the effects of active learning: "Such students who learn to take responsibility for their own learning will help make our society more democratic and a better place for everyone" (p. 17).

Presenting the Fim-Eng praxis, this book has advocated employing diverse forms of art in various educational settings, and propelled scholars and students to produce creative and unconventional works, using art. It has become clear that incorporating artistic practices in education provides educators and learners with freedom to question the norms, that is, what is taken for granted. As Leavy (2015) mentions: "Arts-based practices are on the methodological cutting edge—researchers are *carving* new practices and creating *new ways to see*" (p. 291; original emphasis), I assert that those who are pursuing arts-based approaches hold a massive potential.

Before concluding the discussion, however, let me stress the responsibility of educators/researchers. Barone and Eisner (2012) articulate it clearly:

> ... [T]he ability to use film may very well be one of the important resources for describing and understanding the world or some aspect of it. One of the ramifications of the growth of diversification among forms of representation will be the need in universities and other institutes to prepare individual researchers who possess the skills and talents necessary to do work that is useful.... If videotape becomes a powerful means of addressing the particular circumstances of a particular episode or event, those who use video will need to be able to use it effectively. (p. 169)

In this way, arts-based practitioners should be skilled, innovative, and open to different values. I suggest those who are engaged in filmmaking need to take account of the issues of authority, power, gaze, and representation. At the same time, it is important for the filmmaker to direct her/his attention to the viewers interpreting the intended message diversely. Richard Hickman (2007) explains this point as follows:

> Art-based approaches can be used in both the data gathering phase and the reporting phase, but in the latter there is the added complication of audience interpretation where audiences (or rather, spectators) might be less accustomed to dealing with the interpretation of images. However this could be seen as a strength, in that the 'artist' is not always conscious of the complexity, richness and hidden significance of everything that is created in a given art-work.
> (p. 316)

As Hickman points out here, innovative ways of generating and sharing alternative knowledge emerge from the interactions between arts-based practitioners and their audiences.

Through the presentation of the Film-Eng praxis, this book has urged the readers to practice arts-based approaches in their respective educa-

Conclusion

tional settings. In order to pursue filmmaking in particular, maintaining a critical lens is essential; it enables filmmakers as encoders to challenge the norms and propose alternative perspectives. Jennifer Chan (2008) refers to active global citizens located in Japan, who are striving for the actualization of social justice around the globe:

> The title of this book, *Another Japan Is Possible*, reflects the slogan and frame of mind of some of the alterglobalization activists in Japan, who are part of a larger global justice movement worldwide that rallies around the belief that another world is possible. ... It aims at alternative models of globalization based on transparency, democracy, and participation. (p. 17; original emphasis)

Indeed, the youth in Japan have the tremendous possibilities. The understanding of their native culture(s) and language(s) as well as the skills to handle the English language and digital technology make it possible for the young people to transform themselves into vigorous global citizens and create new views. Now is the time for the young digital generation to get critical, active, and ready for arts-based practices, and carry out self-expression by thinking highly of both the cultural roots and the future routes to take.

序文

　母国日本に戻ってから5年が経つ。アメリカやカナダ、日本などさまざまな国々で生活することで地球市民権（global citizenship）を実践してきた。今、筆者が思うに、地球市民権を行使するには、言語能力、多様なバックグラウンドを持つ人々とコミュニケーションを取ろうとする意思、そして自己を表現する勇気が必要である。
　英語は21世紀に生きる我々にとって必要不可欠である。なぜなら、英語はグローバル言語、すなわち、グローバル化する世界における重要なコミュニケーションの手段だからである。しかし、同時に日本の英語学習者にとって、日本語を駆使できる能力もまた重要である。したがって、本書は二部（第一部が英語、第二部は日本語）で構成されており、バイリンガル方式となっている。
　筆者が研究プロジェクトに従事する大学院生であった頃、政治不安によりカンボジアから日本へ移住した人物に出会った。その人物は、筆者に自己のルーツを忘れることなく、母国である日本の言語文化を大事にするよう教えてくれた。
　日本に戻った今、筆者は、再び日本の文化に向き合い始めた。『無限の網～草間彌生自伝』という著書において、草間（2012）は、「再会した日本語」で自己表現を行う意味を次のように説明している。

> 　1957年の渡米以来、一貫してずっと、私は世界前衛美術画壇の旗手として、美術活動のため渾身闘いぬいて、世界中を東奔西走してきた。その間、当然のことながら、英語で話し、英語でものを考え、一人ごとを言ってきた。
> 　そして私は日本へ帰ってくることにより、長らく使わなかった日本語に再び出会うことになった。日本語を使って小説や詩を書くことで、造形美術ではさぐり得なかった私の存在の別の一面に光をあてて、自己の分野を開拓し、新しい魂の位置に自分を立たせた。(p.238)

同様に筆者も自分の目で、この日本を成す要素を再発見しようと決意した。本書に日本語訳を組み入れるのは、そのような意図によるものである。

　自己のアイデンティティーについて考えると、トランスナショナリティやトランスカルチュラリティといった越境性から離れるのは不可能であると気付く。そのような越境性を帯びた観点から見れば、英語と日本語の間には、簡単に表現することのできない何かが存在すると言える。しかし、映像や音、ことばの組み合わせは、我々の視野を広げ、間に存在する何かを知る助けとなることがわかった。それゆえに容易に表現し得ないものを表す手段として、映像制作を用いるのである。

　そのような間に存在する何かをどうすれば表すことができるのだろうか。筆者が長年疑問に抱いていたことである。しかし、カナダのガルフアイランド・フィルム＆テレビジョンスクールでの学びやブリティッシュ・コロンビア大学において映像制作技術を指導した経験にもとづき、映画における映像や音、ことばの融合による表現は、越境性を帯びた地球市民（global citizen）としての自己にとって非常に重要であると言える。

　日本の若いデジタル世代は、高度な言語能力およびICT技能を身につけた活発な地球市民になる可能性を持っていると、筆者は日本の高等教育に従事して確信した。本書を通じて、能動的な地球市民になるための方法を示したいと願う。

　筆者が心から尊敬する早川敦子先生とジェニファー・チャン先生の激励なしには、本書は成り立たなかったであろう。恩師たちがずっとそうしておられるように、筆者も大切なメッセージを発信していきたいと考えている。また、思慮に富んだ助言をいつも与えてくださる犬塚典子先生に謝意を表したい。アートベース教育・研究のインスピレーションを与えてくださった岡原正幸先生と小倉康嗣先生にもお礼を述べたい。それから、本書の出版に関して、金星堂の横山裕士氏にはお世話になった。最後に、プロジェクトに参加してくれた筆者の大切な生徒全員に感謝する。特に、Ayano、Kanako、Kasumi、Risakoという才能あふれるゼミの学生たち

序文

とともに映画を制作できたこと、そして制作した映画について、Mayu、Miu、Mizuki、Reina、Rina という留学経験者たちから貴重なコメントを得ることができたのは非常に幸運であった。このような思想豊かで、創造力のある学生たちが、筆者に教育者／映像制作者／研究者としての道を切り開いて進むよう力を与えてくれる。少女たち、少年たちよ、地域と世界に羽ばたき、新たな価値観を言葉で、そして視覚的に表現しよう！

原　紘子
2017 年 9 月

Part II: Japanese

Routes to Roots

1
序論：視覚文化と技術

> 新たな歩き方を学びつつ ［中略］
> 私であるというこの映像
> 聞きなさい
> 他者の耳で
> 知らないことを通して知りなさい
> 自分自身になることは他者へとつづく ［後略］
> 　　　　　　　（Trinh T. Minh-ha, 2013, p.177：強調は原文）

　技術の進歩に伴い、デジタルビデオカメラが8ミリや16ミリなどの初期のカメラに取って代わり、映像保存の新たなデバイス（DVD、USBメモリースティック等）がフィルムに代わって用いられている。これらの技術発明が大衆商品となった現在では、ますます多くの人々がデジタルビデオカメラを所有し、映画を制作し、情報共有サイトに自身の作品を公開するようになった。Mirzoeff（1998）は、そのようなムーブメントから視覚文化が生まれ、その発展は「視覚技術」の進歩と切り離すことはできないと指摘する。「視覚技術」という言葉で、Mirzoeffは、「人に観られたり、あるいは、生来の視覚を強化したりするようなあらゆる形式の装置、つまり、油絵にはじまってテレビ、そしてインターネットまで」（p.3）を指している。
　我々は、日本の若者のなかに視覚文化・技術の影響を見ることができる。国立青少年教育振興機構（2015）によれば、調査した高校生の75パーセントが平日にインターネットに接続し、フェイスブック、ライン、ツイッターなどのソーシャル・ネットワーキング・サービス（SNS）を利用するのに1日1時間から6時間以上を費やしているという。日本のこの

ような若者を「デジタル世代」と呼んでもよいだろう。携帯電話やスマートフォンの普及に伴い、人々は写真撮影や録画のためにそういった手軽な機器を使用し、写真や動画をネット上で共有している。そのような動画は「セルフィルム」と呼ばれ、近年研究者たちは、新興の研究題材としてこの新たなデジタル表現に注目してきた（Mitchell, 2016; Moletsane, Mitchell, & Lewin, 2015）。スマートフォン片手に、日本の若者は自由にセルフィルムを制作することができ、視覚文化・技術がめざましく進歩した時代の先頭に立っている。

　そのような若いデジタル世代の出現を背景に、文部科学省（以下、文科省）は 2013 年 6 月、『第 2 期教育振興基本計画』を発表した。この計画で文科省は、「グローバル化が進み産業化された社会においては、英語およびメディアリテラシーが必要不可欠になっている」（2013a）と述べた。このように、文科省は「英語およびメディアリテラシー」という 2 つの要素を、将来を担う世代に必須のものと明記している。本書では、若者がこれらの要素を身につけるには、教育にアート（芸術）を組み入れることが必要であると主張する。『平成 25 年度文部科学白書』において、文科省はアートの重要性を次のように述べている。

> 2020 年までの目標の一つとしては、芸術および文化が根付き、アーティスト、若者、文化人、学者が日本を訪れるように引きつける国際文化交流の中心となるような魅力のある国に日本をすることである。もう一つの目標は、新たな価値観が生み出されるような芸術および文化が根付いた国家として、また、芸術および文化によって支えられた円熟した社会に向けた新たな模範として、日本を世界に示すことである。（2013b）

このように、現在ではアートが将来における新たな価値観の出現と普及のカギを握っていると考えられている。

　これは、教育においてアートを重視することの意義を主張する研究者たち（たとえば、Dewey, 1934; Eisner, 1972; Frank, 1966; Lewis, 1976）の貢献に起因する新たな傾向である。科学が社会で台頭する一方、Dewey

(1934) は、「アートは、グラフや統計値にはない予測のモードであり、規則や指針、勧告や管理にはない人間関係の可能性をほのめかす」(p.349) と述べ、科学とは異なるアートの重要性に注目するよう人々に促している。Frank (1966) もまた、科学主導の社会におけるアートの存在を重要視しており、「アートは、教育プログラムに不可欠で喫緊に必要とされており、そこに完全に受け入れられるのを待っている」(p.459) と述べている。

　アートを教育に組み込む重要性を強調しつつ、研究者たちは、アートが学校だけでなく社会全体においても軽視されている問題の根源を探ってきた。これに関して、Dewey (1934) は有用な分析をし、二分法に言及している。

> 我々の由緒ある遺産の精神的・観念的要素と、科学によって明らかにされている物質性の構造の間に存在している対立は、デカルトとロック以降の哲学により体系立てられた二元論の根源である。(p.338)

Dewey はこのように、科学と芸術のあいだに隔壁を造っている二元的システムが古くから存在すると論じている。Dewey が論じた二項対立に関連し、Eisner (1972) は、「プラトンが頭脳労働と手仕事を区別し、後者よりも前者により高い善性を与えて以来、アートがどちらの分野に属するかが問題にされることはほとんどなかった」(p.262) と述べ、ギリシャ哲学の影響を指摘した。このような二元構造に関して、Lewis (1976) は、それを超越する方法を提案した。

> 私がここで提案しているのは、人々が自然環境と社会環境にどのように対処しているかが美術と人文学、科学に相互補完的に表れていると考えること、情動と認知を切り離している障壁を取り除くこと、美術とその他の学問分野を結びつける基本的な工程に美術指導を統合することによりカリキュラムを改革することである。(p.168)

ここでルイスは、学問分野間の境界と「情動／認知」などの二項対立の関連を示し、あらゆる科目が調和するような新たな枠組みをカリキュラムに取り入れる必要性を指摘している。

　近年、学者たちは、多様な芸術様式を教育や研究の中に組み入れた「アートベース（arts-based）」と呼ばれるモデルを提示してきた（Barone & Eisner, 2012; Eisner, 2002; Hickman, 2007; Leavy, 2015; Siegesmund & Cahnmann-Taylor, 2008）。Eisner（2002）はアートの重要性を次のように強調する。

> アートにおいて、楽譜の解釈や、絵画や彫刻を説明する方法は一つではなく、ダンスパフォーマンスの正しいフォームや、人物や状況に関する詩的表現の意味も一つではない。アートでは多様性と変異性が中心に置かれる。これは、教育がアートから学ぶことのできる一つの教訓である。（p.197）

このようにEisnerは、教育および研究にアートを活用することを奨励し、それにより多様な考え方が生じると主張している。Leavy（2015）は、この新たな方法論の特質を以下のように説明している。

> <u>アートベース・リサーチの実践</u>は、データ生成、分析、解釈、表現を含む、社会に関する研究のすべての段階において、学問分野によらず研究者たちが使用する方法論的手段の一式である。これらの新興の手段は、理論と実践を結びつけた包括的で結合的な方法で社会に関する研究議題を扱うために、創造的芸術の理念を適合させている。（p.4、強調は原文）

したがって、アートベース・メソッドは、前述の二項対立を超越するだけでなく、「理論」と「実践」を融合するのに有用である。Barone & Eisner（2012）は、アートベース・アプローチには幅広い可能性があると考えている。

> アートベース・リサーチを行っている研究者は、因習的な見方を強化することにより、これら［社会的、文化的］現象について普及している憶測を確固とするために貢献するかわりに、異なる方向から世界について再考し、新鮮な見方を通して知り、それによって唯一の正統な視点（POV）に疑問を投げかけるよう、読者あるいは作品を見る人（アーティスト自身も含む）を説得することができる。(p.16、強調は原文；[ ]の挿入は筆者による)

ここで Barone & Eisner が指摘するのは、アートベース実践はただ一つの絶対的な知識を生成する伝統的な方法を廃止し、当然と考えられていることに対し批判的に検証する姿勢をもつ良い機会を与えてくれるということである。

　これらの学者の主張に鑑み、現代のデジタル化の波を背景として、本書ではアートベース実践例を提示して、授業でアートを活用することで広がる可能性について探る。一口にアートと言っても、絵画、彫刻、歌唱、楽器演奏、演劇、パフォーマンス、ブログ作成、写真撮影、映画制作など、その形式はじつに多様である。本書では、映画制作に焦点を当て、指導および学習環境に映画制作を取り入れることの意義について論じる。この目的を達成するため、授業に視覚的表現（絵コンテや映画制作）と英語使用を伴うフィルム－イング（Film-Eng）実践（praxis（ギリシャ語）：「プラクシス」）を導入する。Film-Eng とは、映画制作（Filming）と英語（English）の二つの語を合わせたものであり、本書が提示する新造語である。このプラクシスをアートの一形式かつ芸術的実践、すなわち、アートベース・アプローチとみなす。そして、これがさまざまな教育現場において認識・実践されるべきであることを主張する。本書では、フィルミングとフィルムメイキングは、どちらも映画制作を意味する。本書で提示するように、フィルム－イング実践を通じて創造的な表現を授業に取り入れることは、英語力とクリティカル・メディアリテラシーを涵養し、デコーディングとエンコーディングの能力を強化するのに役立つ。本書でいうデコーディングとは、メディアが構築し流通させるメッセージを解釈することである。エ

ンコーディングとは、自己表現のために言語（英語や日本語）を使用し、メッセージを伝達することである。

　本書は、フィルム－イング実践がどのように授業で行われるかを具体的に示し、この新たな教育実践が、英語を外国語として学ぶ日本の英語（EFL）学習者に役立つものであることを示す。本書は、第一部が英語、第二部は日本語で論じる二部構成であり、それぞれが15ユニットから成る。第一部ユニット2では、加速するグローバル化やデジタル化に対応するために必要となる多様なリテラシー（クリティカル・メディアリテラシーを含む）を紹介する。続いてユニット3と4では、日本とカナダにおいてメディア教育がどのように概念化されているかについて論じる。ユニット5では、日本とカナダの教育政策を裏打ちする理論的な基盤を示す。ユニット6では、Hall に言及しつつデコーディングの意味を探り、ジェンダー、人種、民族に関するさまざまな表象を批判的な視点から分析する方法を提示する。ユニット7から10では、エンコーディングに必要となる4つの工程、すなわち、アクティブ・ラーニング、撮影技術、絵コンテ、映像撮影・編集について説明する。ユニット11では、大学の授業に応用できるフィルム－イング実践について説明し、この実践を実際に経験した学生たちの声を紹介する。筆者の指導する学生が『幽玄』という短編映画を制作したが、その脚本をユニット12で紹介する。ユニット13は、この映画の基礎をなす概念、および映画制作者として学生たちが視聴者に伝えようとしたことについて説明する。ユニット14では、『幽玄』を視聴した学生たちのコメントを参照しつつ、観客によって行われる多様なデコーディング方法について論じる。そして最終ユニットでは、研究結果とそれについての考察、アートベース・アプローチとしてのフィルム－イング実践の意義についてまとめる。本書では、プライバシー保護のため、生徒たちの名前をそれぞれが決めた仮名で表記する。

　フィルム－イング実践は適切に実施されれば、教育者と学習者の両方に多くの可能性を開く。本書は、理論・方法論・政策の面でメディア教育やアートベース教育、教育政策研究に貢献するだろう。理論的な面では、本

書では、デコーディング（メッセージの受信・解釈）とエンコーディング（メッセージの創作・発信）の関係についての我々の理解を深める。方法論的には、アートベース・アプローチとしてのフィルム－イング実践がもつ大きな可能性を裏付けるため、質的研究方法と視覚的研究方法を結合させた新たな方法を採用する。政策面では、クリティカル・メディアリテラシー促進のための教育における言説と実践のギャップを示し、それにより、他の教育機関における類似プロジェクトの概念化と実施を啓発する。

2
グローバル化とデジタル化に対応するリテラシー

　リテラシーについては、教育学、言語学、心理学、文化人類学、社会学、歴史学など、広範な学問領域の学者によって研究がなされてきた。本書は、英語とクリティカル・メディアリテラシーの2つのリテラシーに注目する。第一に、英語は概して日本社会においてますます重要になってきている。特に英語によるコミュニケーション能力は欠かせない。これは、日本政府による『日本再生戦略』(2014)が「実践的な英語教育を促進する」(p.72)と唱えていることからも明らかである。

　教育におけるこのような変化は、グローバル言語としての英語の台頭によるものである。日本では多くの大学生が卒業必須科目として英語授業を履修している。事実、『グローバル化に対応した英語教育改革実施計画』にみられるように、文科省は小学校・中学校・高等学校レベルでの英語教育を促進することにより、「日本における新しい英語教育の大規模展開」(文科省、2013c)を目ざしている。このような新たな語学教育に関して、文科省はそのプランを以下のように具体的に説明している。

> 新たな英語教育のスタイルとして、プランは次の3点により、確実に英語コミュニケーション能力を増進する。(1) 小学3、4年次での英語活動および5、6年次での教科としての英語学習、(2) 中学校での英語授業を英語で行い、高等学校ではプレゼンテーションやディベートに焦点を当てることで、英語教育の目標と内容の水準を上げる、(3) 小学校、中学校、高等学校を通じて一貫した学習目標を確立する。(2013b)

要するに、21世紀に求められるリテラシーの一つが英語で考えを述べる能力であり、英語力は日本に暮らす若者に必要不可欠なものとされている。

次に、本書で論じるもう一つのリテラシーはクリティカル・メディアリテラシーである。視覚文化とテクノロジーの発展に伴い、リテラシーの概念は変化してきた。「マルチリテラシー」という用語を使って、Tannenbaum & Goldstein（2005）は、リテラシーは「書き言葉や話し言葉だけでなく、視覚、音声、空間、行動など、意味を形成するもろもろの形態に関係」（p.124）があると述べている。テクノロジーの進歩に対応するのに必要な能力は、「メディアリテラシー」、「ビジュアルリテラシー」（Chauvin, 2003）、「インフォメーションリテラシー」（Ragains, 2006）、「ビジュアル・メディアリテラシー」（Duffelmeyer, 2004）、「デジタルリテラシー」（Tyner, 2003）など多様な用語で表現され論じられてきた。Chauvin（2003）によれば、メディアリテラシーとビジュアルリテラシーに関して、この2つが同一のものなのかどうかが学者の間で議論になってきた。Chauvin は、両者の違いについて調査し、メディアリテラシーはマスメディアに関連する種々の能力（評価や伝達）であり、ビジュアルリテラシーにはメッセージを創作する能力が含まれるとした。

学者たちによってリテラシーについてのさまざまな見解が提唱されてきたが、それらには「マスメディアに、そして、どのように何の目的でメッセージが構築され、大衆に消費されているかに、重点を置いている」（Chauvin, 2003, p.122、強調は原文）という共通点がある。Ragains（2006）は、インフォメーションリテラシーについての有用な定義を提唱し、それは「情報を識別し、確認し、有効に利用する能力である。この定義は、批判的思考とインフォメーションテクノロジーの機能を結合させている」（p.4）と述べた。Walter（1999）が、「一般的な意見においても学術的な理論においても、リテラシーについて簡潔で普遍的な定義はない」（p.32）と述べたように、現在では、リテラシーについての多様な見方が存在し、デジタル時代における新たな見解が出現し続けている。

ここでのリテラシーに関する議論から明らかになるのは、分析し、批判的に考え、自力でメッセージを生み出すという3つの能力がさまざまな定義の根底にあるということである。これらの研究者の主張を取り入れ、

本書では、「クリティカル・メディアリテラシー」という用語を用いることにする。この新たなリテラシーと英語力を養成する教育方法を提示し、どのように他の高等教育機関で実施できるかを提示するのが本書のねらいである。Hartley (2007) は、高等教育の可能性を次のように述べている。

> ……知識基盤社会における転換と成長の主体として、高等教育は、独創的革新を展開する（あるいは放つ）ための力、言い換えれば、グローバルな状況下の国家間競争に関心を持つあらゆる国において、諸問題を国家政策レベルにまで引き上げる可能性となり得る。(p.139)

このように、高等教育機関は、若者を自ら考え行動するように導く重要な役割を果たしている。

2020年の東京でのオリンピック・パラリンピックに伴い、文科省は、日本の教育ビジョンについて次のように示している。

> 国際社会の加速するグローバル化の真っただ中で日本の成長を維持する将来に向けて、迅速な発展をすすめるには、日本の成長を牽引し世界を舞台に多様な分野で活躍するグローバル人材を育成し、豊かな言語およびコミュニケーション能力、自立、主張、そして、日本文化についての深い理解ならびに日本人としてのアイデンティティーを前提に他の文化を理解できる思考を養うことは喫緊の課題である。2020年の東京オリンピック・パラリンピックを主催することは、世界の目が日本に向けられる良い機会であるが、同時に重大な転機であり、世界を舞台として活躍し、諸問題をグローバルな視点から考察する人材を育成する必要がある。(2013b)

ここで述べられているように、英語力とクリティカル・メディアリテラシーは、現在のグローバル化とデジタル化の速度に対応するために必要不可欠な能力である。先述のように、本書は、これらの能力を身につける一つの方法として、フィルム－イング実践を提唱する。その実践活動について詳述する前に、以下のユニットではそれぞれ、日本とカナダにおけるメデ

ィア教育に注目する。両者の比較を通して、学校教育においてリテラシーがどのように養成されているか、そして、その教育実践の根底にある概念的枠組みについて考察する。

3
日本におけるメディア教育

　本ユニットでは、日本において、メディア教育がどのように概念化され、どのようなリテラシーを身につけることが奨励されているのかについてみていく。デジタル技術、言い換えれば、情報コミュニケーション技術（ICT）あるいは情報技術（IT）を、日本のメディア教育から切り離すことはできない。前のユニットで説明したように、学生たちの英語力強化を目ざしつつ、日本は情報教育と呼ばれるメディア教育を通じてICTリテラシーの開発に重きを置いてきた。これは、「日本が情報革命において世界をリードして」（Pharr, 1996, p.4）きた歴史的背景によるものである。

　ICT能力は21世紀に生きる国民に必要不可欠であると考え、日本政府は2001年、「高度情報通信ネットワーク社会推進戦略本部（IT総合戦略本部）」を内閣に設立した。当部は2009年、『i-Japan戦略2015〜国民主役の「デジタル安心・活力社会」の実現を目指して〜』という国家方針を発表した。これは、デジタル技術がもたらす日本社会へのプラス効果について以下のように述べている。

> ……デジタル技術と情報は、経済ならびに社会を通じて、デジタル革新および新たな活力を導く。そこでは、自発的かつ進歩的な創作および革新を始めるために［中略］、そして、企業が低コストならびに高利益構造へ転換し、持続可能な経済成長と環境資源の制約の平衡が保たれ、国際社会との提携、協力、共存が達成される社会をつくるために、人々と社会全体がこの新たな活力をいかすことができる。(p.2)

IT総合戦略本部はさらに、そのような社会を実現できる「高度なデジタル技術力を持つ人材」（p.16）を育成するには、「情報教育の内容を改良し、

拡張すること」(p.16) が理想的だと述べている。IT総合戦略本部が、国民がICTについての徹底的な知識を身につけることが日本経済および社会の活性化に必要だと考えていることは、当方針から明らかである。

　この流れに応じて、文科省 (2011) は『教育の情報化ビジョン〜21世紀にふさわしい学びと学校の創造を目指して〜』という方針書で、いかにICTの知識と技能を国民に普及するかについてまとめた。それによると、文科省が情報教育により伸ばすことを目ざしている能力は次のものである。

> ……情報を活用する実践的能力（必要な情報を自分で収集、判断、処理、整頓、創造、表現し、受信者の状況にあわせて情報を送信、伝達する能力、また、問題や目的にあわせて情報源を適切に活用する能力も含む）。(p.9)

ここから明らかなのは、上記の能力を身につけるように生徒を教育し、ICTを駆使して、彼らが受信者から知識の発信者／制作者に成長するよう促すことを、文科省が推奨しているということである。

　文科省は情報教育を通じてICTリテラシーを継続的に促進してきたが、その間、日本を取り巻く状況は変化してきた。IT総合戦略本部 (2013) は『世界最先端IT国家創造宣言』のなかで、「国際的な視点から見ると、日本は世界を牽引するIT国家としての地位を失い、国際競争力ランキングにおいて多くの国々が日本を上回った」(p.3) と述べ、状況の変化を認識している。こういった現状を打開し、日本の地位を取り戻すために、IT総合戦略本部は次のような戦略を述べている。

> ……教育環境（ソフトウェアおよびハードウェアを含むインフラ設備）のデジタル化、全国民のITリテラシーの増進、機会の提供（環境を推奨し、個々の能力を高める挑戦的な活動を奨励すること）を通じた、将来の革新を率先できるような世界トップレベルのIT人材の育成、そして、特定のカリキュラム（特定のニーズや教育目標のために準備したカ

リキュラム）を用いた情報教育を行う。（p.26）

IT 総合戦略本部は、すべての国民が ICT を使いこなせるようになるには、小学校・中学校・高等学校の各レベルで生徒たちの ICT 技能を高めることが必要だとしている。

　デジタル技術の活用に焦点を当てるメディア教育（むしろ日本の場合は、情報教育と呼ぶ方がよいであろう）は、独創的な作品制作やアートの表現形式としてコンピューター技術を用いるアーティストたちの、世代を超えた輩出を可能にしている。日本では、アートとコンピューターサイエンスの結合が、いわゆるデジタルメディアアーティストの作品において顕著である。Ippolito（2007）は「アヴァンギャルドから――日本におけるデジタルメディアアートの文化的起源の再概念化――」の中で、「科学技術的なメディア、たとえば、電気ベル、光、遠隔制御装置など」（p.150）を使用した 1980 年代以降の主要なデジタルメディアアーティスト 3 名（藤幡正樹、河口洋一郎、土佐尚子）に言及している。Ippolito は、コンピューターグラフィックスやアルゴリズムなどのコンピューター技術が、彼らの芸術作品においていかに重要な役割を果たしているかを調査し、テクノロジーとアートが融合し、芸術作品として共存できる可能性を提示している。

　日本の場合、デジタル技術を重視することで、結果として、教育を通じた ICT リテラシーの発達や、表現様式としてテクノロジーを用いることのできる人材の開発がもたらされている。文科省は ICT に注目しつつ、世界中で加速するデジタル化とグローバル化に対応するため、新たな教育方法を提示している。

> 今後、教育は、一方向の指導（すなわち講義）あるいは集団授業を通じてだけでなく、ICT を活用することにより進歩すべきであり、それは、生きる意志、学ぶ意志、知的好奇心を十分に啓発することを目指し、生徒一人一人の能力や特技に合った授業を通じて基礎的な知識および技能

を修得し、生徒同士がともに学び、また、さまざまなことを体験するために周囲、あるいは、海外の人々との協力により、生徒たちが諸問題を認識し取り組むことができるような新たな学習方法を取り入れるためである。(2013a)

この声明が言わんとするのは、双方向型教育、言い換えれば、アクティブラーニング（後で詳述）が、日本の学校において緊急に必要とされており、この新しい教育を進める上でICTが主要な役割を果たすということである。このように、情報教育の領域を越えて、指導と学習に関わるさまざまな面でICT統合を重視しようという新しい傾向が見られる。次のユニットでは、日本国外でメディア教育はどのように概念化されているのかについて、カナダの例に注目して考える。

4
カナダにおけるメディア教育

　テレビは、外部のもの（それに伴う危険や猛威）を我々の家庭の平和の中に持ち込む。（Marshall McLuhan, 1988a, p.148）

　このユニットでは、カナダの首都オタワが位置するオンタリオ州で行われている教育を紹介する。オンタリオ教育省（以下、OME）は、学問分野の枠を超えて ICT を活用することの重要性を主張している。『オンタリオ・カリキュラム 1－8 学年：科学とテクノロジー』は、「学習支援およびコミュニケーションのために、生徒たちの ICT 利用を適宜促進すべきである」（OME, 2007, p.41）と明言している。この叙述は、『科学技術教育』（9－12 学年）、『言語』（1－8 学年）、『英語』（9－12 学年）、『美術』（1－12 学年）などのカリキュラムに共通して見られる。OME（2009a）は、ICT 技能の修得が教育において奨励される理由について、次のように説明する。

　　生徒たちは競争的なグローバル経済に完全に参加し、環境的に弱い世界において責任を果たせる国民になるのを可能にする技術的能力および知識を身につける必要がある。現在の社会において成功するためには、生徒たちは実践的な問題解決者ならびに批判的思考者であることが必要で、理解し、疑問を持ち、技術革新がもたらすものに対応する能力がなくてはならない。（p.3）

　ICT 技能の修得が先述の科目分野において必要不可欠だと考えているのに加えて、OME は批判的思考ならびにクリティカル・リテラシーを学際的に養う必要性も力説している。たとえば、『オンタリオ・カリキュラ

ム1-8学年：美術』には、「クリティカル・リテラシーを身につけた生徒たちは、あるテキストが打ち出す世界観はどのようなものか、その考えは容認できるものか、そのテキストによって利益を得るのはだれか、そして、読者はどのような影響を受けるのかと問いかけながら批判的な姿勢を取り入れる」（2009b, p.53）と述べられており、クリティカル・リテラシーが生徒たちにとっていかに役立つかが示されている。この叙述は、9-12学年向けの美術カリキュラムに共通して見られる。さらに、『オンタリオ・カリキュラム9-10学年：英語』は、クリティカル・リテラシーのもう一つの特徴についても述べている。

> クリティカル・リテラシーは、問いかけや現状への挑戦を伴い、生徒たちが社会における権力や正義に関わる諸問題を考察できるよう導く。この教育プログラムでは、自己表現を行い、強い影響を受けている諸問題について思い切って意見を述べられるようにすることにより、生徒たちに力を与える。（2007b, p.34）

このように、教育分野においては、ICT技能とクリティカル・リテラシーは同様に重要だと考えられていることが、これらの叙述からわかる。

じつはOMEは、「多様なリテラシー」の指導ならびに学習を促進している。クリティカル・リテラシーだけでなく、機能的リテラシーや数的リテラシー、メディアリテラシーなどが含まれる。OMEは特に生徒たちのメディアリテラシーの養成を重点的に行っている。このことは、『オンタリオ・カリキュラム：言語』および『オンタリオ・カリキュラム：英語』において顕著である。たとえば、『オンタリオ・カリキュラム：言語』では、「このカリキュラムは、生徒たちがオーラル・コミュニケーション、リーディング、ライティング、メディアリテラシーという4つの要素、あるいは、広範囲の学習分野において、教養を身につけるために必要となる知識と技能を体系づけている。これらの学習分野には緊密な相互関係がある」（2006, pp.4-5）と述べられている。そして、クリティカル・リテラシーとメディアリテラシーを培う手段として、メディア教育が実践されている。

研究者たちはカナダのメディア教育が進んでいることを指摘している（Anderson, Duncan, & Pungente, 2001; Duncan, 2005 参照）。Anderson, Duncan, & Pungente（2001）は、カナダの学校でメディア教育がうまく実施されているのは、ナショナリズムや国家のアイデンティティーを維持する必要性に起因すると論じている。カナダでは、「アメリカのポップカルチャーの普及についての深刻な懸念」（Anderson et al., 2001, p.33）があると言う。加えて、メディア研究で名高い McLuhan はカナダにおけるメディア教育の発展に貢献した。McLuhan は、「ニューメディア、たとえば、電話、電報、ラジオ、テレビ」（1988b, p.45）が人々の日常生活や見たり聞いたりする体験を劇的に変えたと指摘した。マスメディアに関する McLuhan の研究は、その後のメディア理論に大きな影響を与えた。メディアの役目と視聴者に及ぼす影響についての活発な議論は、1960 年代以降のメディア教育の実践と新たな教育政策の形成に影響を与えた。メディアリテラシー指導の緊急性は、メディア教育を学校のカリキュラムに組み入れると制定したカナダ州政府の行動に見てとれる（Anderson et al., 2001）。なかでもオンタリオ州は、「メディアリテラシーを幼稚園から高校までカリキュラムの必須項目とした北米初の管轄区」（Duncan, 2005, p.3）である。

メディアリテラシーとは、「メディアの本質、メディアが使用する技術、そして、それらの技術による効果についての知識および批判的理解」であり、「マスメディアを理解し、積極的かつ批判的に活用できる能力」（OME, 2007c, p.211）と定義されている。また、OME はメディアの主要な特性を、次のように 5 つ提示している。

1. すべてのメディアは作られたものである。
2. メディアは信念や価値基準のメッセージを包含する。
3. 人はメッセージをさまざまに解釈する。
4. メディアには特別な利益（営利的、イデオロギー的、政治的）がある。

5. それぞれの媒体は固有の言葉、スタイル、形式、技術、しきたり、美的感覚を持つ。（2007c, p.211）

OMEは、「これらのメディア（たとえば、インターネット、映画、テレビ）が我々の生活や社会に及ぼす力や広い影響」（2007b, p.18、OMEの表現を用いて括弧内追加は筆者）があることから、メディア教育の実践およびメディアリテラシー促進の必要性を認めている。

　確かに英語のカリキュラムでは、「文学研究とメディア研究は、人種差別、性差別、あるいは、同性愛嫌悪として現れるようないじめ、暴力、差別が個人や家庭に及ぼす社会的、感情的な影響について探求する貴重な機会を生徒と教師両方に与えてくれる」（2007b, p.34）という叙述があり、メディア教育の重要性が強調されている。このように、カナダ・オンタリオ州の場合、OMEはICTリテラシー、クリティカル・リテラシー、メディアリテラシーを含む「多様なリテラシー」を強化する必要性を認識している。『科学とテクノロジー』『科学技術教育』『言語』『英語』『美術』などのOMEのカリキュラムは、これらのリテラシーを育成する活動に明確な指針と助言を提供しており、教師が効果的な指導案を作成するためだけでなく、生徒たちが次第に「批判的な」観客ならびに制作者になることを学ぶ上で助けとなる。

5
批判的思考

　本ユニットでは、日本とカナダの教育政策の裏にある理論的な基盤を明らかにする。日本とカナダのオンタリオにおけるメディア教育の事例から、論ずるべきいくつかの相違点と類似点が浮かび上がってくる。国家のアジェンダと世界における立場の違いにより、両国には明らかな相違がある。ここでは、そのような相違点は別にして、前述したリテラシーの3つの重要なポイント、つまり、分析し、批判的に考え、自力でメッセージを生み出すという能力に関して、日本とカナダにはどのような類似点と相違点とがあるのかについてみてゆく。オンタリオで実践されている教育では、明らかに上記の3つの要素が根底にある。分析、批判的思考、創造性に重点を置くオンタリオの教育モデルは、構築主義理論と批判的教育学の結合を示している。

　日本の教育にも構築主義の大きな影響がみられる。デジタル技術とその革新を先導する国家となるため、日本は教育を通じたICTリテラシーの促進に全力を尽くしてきた。デジタルメディアを活用し、情報教育の授業を受ける学生たちは、問題解決能力を修得することを奨励されている。前述の日本の教育目標は、「生徒の知識の生産、生徒の知識の明示、生徒の声や選択肢の拡大」(Tyner, 2003, p.383) という構築主義的学習の目的と一致する。このように、構築主義理論にもとづく教育は、生徒が「自分の知識をさまざまな方法で表現し、問題を解決し、自身の作業結果を見直し、知識を構築する」(Ivers & Barron, 2006, p.3) ことを手助けすることを目ざすものである。教育を通じて分析力と情報発信能力を育成する重要性を認識する日本と、ICTリテラシーを含む多様なリテラシーを啓発するオンタリオは共に、「生徒と教師がアクセスし、分析し、調査し、多様

なメディアと情報を用いてさまざまな方法でものを作り出す」(Tyner, 2003, p.383)ことを促進する構築主義的指導および学習モデルに従っている部分があると考えてよいだろう。

しかし、日本の事例とは違い、「批判的」ならびに「批判的に」という言葉がオンタリオの教育目標の中ではひんぱんに使用されていることがわかる。これは、Freire (2003) が提唱した批判的教育学の影響によるものである。不均衡な権力構造を維持する支配的で抑圧的なシステムに対抗して、Freire は、「まず人々はその原因を批判的に認知しなければならず、行動を変えることで、新たな状態を生み出すことができる」(p.47) と主張し、批判的思考の重要性を説いている。批判的思考という用語により、Freire は「現実を静的な存在というよりはむしろ過程、変化するものと知覚する思考、換言すると、行動と分離しない思考」(2003, p.92) を意味している。ここで Freire は、学習者が公平な社会を目ざす活発な参与者になれるよう、教育を通じて批判的思考を涵養する必要性を主張している。

Freire の主張を支持しつつ、hooks (2003) は教室で啓発するリテラシーは批判的思考に至ると論じる。インタビュー番組での応答を振り返り、hooks は批判的思考の意義について次のように強調した。

> 私は、自分にとって「批判的思考」は、変化の可能性をもたらす基本要素だと答えた。階級、人種、ジェンダー、あるいは、社会的身分が何であろうとも、自分自身や自己の生活を批判的に考察する能力がなければ、誰も前進し、変化し、成長することはできないという自分の信念を語った。(p.202)

このように hooks は、21 世紀に生きる人々にとって批判的思考は必要不可欠なものだと示している。さらに、Lankshear & Knobel (2005) は、批判的思考の実用的な機能について以下のように詳述している。

> 批判的思考は、社会において自己が置かれた地位の根本的原因、つまり、我々個人の生活に関する社会経済的、政治的、文化的、歴史的状況

を知覚することから始まる。しかし、批判的思考は知覚を超え、人々が自己の人生を形づくり管理するために起こす行動や下す決断へと続く。
(p.299)

このように、批判的思考は、人が自分のまわりの環境を意識し、より大きな状況に自らを関連づけ、さらに、思考を行動に変えるよう促す重要な知的活動である。オンタリオの事例に見られるように、批判的教育学の影響を受けたメディア教育は、批判的思考の強化を目的の中心に据え、学習者が自己を取り囲むメディアのメッセージや表象について批判的に考えるよう奨励している。そうすることで、学習者は「批判的な（クリティカル）」メディアリテラシーの獲得に至るのである。

教育を通じたクリティカル・メディアリテラシーの養成は、デジタル化とグローバル化が加速する時代において必須である。Semali（2000）は、クリティカル・メディアリテラシーの有用性を以下のように明瞭に説明している。

> 女性、マイノリティー、他文化の人々、民族集団に関する文や映像および他の社会集団に関する映像についての分析ならびに批評は、固定観念、軽蔑的な偏見、差別を取り出し、暴露し、認識するために重要である。また、このような行いにより、これらの文や映像がいかに我々の体験やアイデンティティー構築の手伝いをしているのかを気付かせ理解させてくれる。(p.33)

このように、教育におけるクリティカル・メディアリテラシーの養成は、視覚に訴える現在の事象に対応する手段として極めて重要であり、それにより日常生活における批判的思考の実践が可能になる。学校教育によるクリティカル・メディアリテラシーの強化により、批判的思考が行動を導くのと同じように、学習者が新しい考えを生み出す制作者として自己を変えるよう、インスピレーションが与えられる可能性がある。ここでの議論にもとづき、次のユニットでは、メディアのメッセージと表象を分析する際の批判的視点の活用方法について述べる。

6
デコーディング：批判的分析
（ジェンダー、人種、民族）

　カルチュラル・スタディーズ（文化研究）の著名な研究者 Hall（1999）は、テレビが視聴者に及ぼす影響について探究した。ホールによると、制作者と視聴者の間には、エンコーディングとデコーディングという工程が存在している。この Hall の主張については、詳細な研究が行われた（Hara, 2014 参照のこと）。エンコーディングとデコーディングは映像撮影においてカギとなる重要な概念である。映像にある種のメッセージを込めるとき、それは、「生産、循環、流通、消費、再生産」（Hall, 1999, p.508）という 5 つの要素をもつマスメディアにより支配的な意味が作り出され、大衆に向けて送信される。視聴者は、メディアにより生産されたメッセージを受信し解釈または解読する。Hall は、視聴者の解釈は、制作者の意図と必ずしも一致するとは限らないと指摘する。本書では、このような視聴者と制作者間の不一致について後に深く考察する。Hall の批判的分析から明らかになったのは、視聴者はマスメディアにより作り出されるメッセージを批判的に解読することが必要だということである。要するに、「どのようなメッセージが伝達されているのか」「誰がそのメッセージを創作／挿入しているのか」「生産されたメッセージの裏にはどのような意図があるのか」「そのメッセージを送信する対象は誰か」と問うことが重要である。このような問いかけをすることで、批判的思考の習慣が身につくのである。

　我々はさまざまなメディアに囲まれており、批判的思考を日々実践する必要がある。批判的な視点を用いて解読する方法を理解するために、ここ

で民族誌映画の先駆者であるFlahertyの映像作品を分析してみよう。カナダの厳寒地方に住む先住民の暮らしをとらえたFlahertyの『極北のナヌーク』(1922) は、文化人類学者の間で論争の的となった。特に、作品の中のナレーションの使用についての論争は注目に値する。民族誌映画における字幕を使用したナレーション技術を発明したとして、Flahertyを称賛する学者もいる。たとえば、MacDougall (2006) は以下のように述べている。

> Flahertyの映画は、[中略] 当時の文化人類学において前例のないナレーション方法を民族誌に提案した。民族誌学者がのちに何年もかけて発表する「ライフヒストリー」のように、彼の映画は、いかにさまざまな社会的影響が社会生活を営む個人に収束するかを把握する唯一の方法がナレーションであると示した。(p.233)

この16ミリカメラで撮影された無声映画において、Flahertyは自身が観察し、共に過ごした先住民についての話を視聴者に伝える手段として説明字幕を使った。このFlahertyのナレーション使用については、問題点を指摘する学者もいる。Russell (1999) は次のように述べている。

> 映画言語に精通しているFlahertyの自然な物語風のリアリズム<u>のために</u>、彼は映画のシーンのねつ造、言い換えれば、上演劇のリアリスト的要素に確実性を持たせたとして非難され得る。このようなリアリズムは、イヌイットの人々の演技および彼らが演じるように依頼された日常生活劇によって駆り立てられる。(p.110、強調は原文)

このように、学者たちは、先住民の暮らしを伝えるためにFlahertyが字幕を使用したことにより、「現実」や「真実」を叙述する権威としての民族誌学者の主観性が強まり、撮影する民族誌学者とエキゾチックな存在として撮影される先住民との間に不平等な二極的関係が持続されると批判した。したがって、「Flahertyが登場人物に与えた主観性は、[中略] ごくわ

ずかである」(Russell, 1999, p.109) とされている。

　さらに、フェミニズム学者たちは、女性らしさと男性らしさの構築と、映画の登場人物がどのように男性あるいは女性としての意味づけをされているかについて、考察する必要があると論じた。たとえば、Pink（2007）は、性別役割を与えられたアイデンティティーの構築について次のように述べている。

> ……研究者と情報提供者の両者が性別役割を与えられた個人として、どのように自己および互いを体験するかは、両者が参加する特有の折衝次第である。視覚的イメージやテクノロジーが研究プロジェクトの一部であるならば、それらは研究者と情報提供者両方のアイデンティティーがどのように構築され解釈されるかに影響を及ぼす。(p.26)

Flaherty の映画の場合、タイトルが示すように、カメラはナヌークという男性がイグルーと呼ばれるスノーハウスを建てる様子など、彼の動作に注目する。ナヌークの配偶者であるナイラが映像に登場する前には、「ナイラ～ほほえむひと～」というタイトルが現れ、ほほえんでいる女性が登場する。ナヌークが野外で行うさまざまな活動が描写される一方、ナイラが赤ちゃんを抱っこしたり、赤ちゃんに寄り添ったりする場面が映し出される。性別役割を与えられたアイデンティティーの構築について考察するフェミニズム研究者は、映画で描かれる性別による役割分業はそもそも先住民のライフスタイルの一部であるのか、あるいは、映画制作者によってさまざまな活動が性別役割を与えられ組み立てられているのか、視聴者に熟考するよう促している。

　さらに、視線の問題は、フェミニズム映画理論によって指摘されている（Hara, 2014 参照）。シネマにおける女性らしさの構築と表象に関する精神分析の先駆者である Doane (1982) は、いかに女性らしさが男性の視線にとって心地よいオブジェとしての役目を果たしてきたかを指摘している。Doane は、見る力を持つ男性と見られるオブジェとしての女性の二

項対立を維持する家父長制を疑問視する。映画に見られる理想的な女性らしさを強化している支配的なシステムを脱構築するために、Doaneは女性に見る力を持たせる「女性観客性」という概念を提唱した。この概念をFlahertyの映画に適用すると、観客は、映画制作者が権威として位置している権力構造の下に、その権威によって制限された行為主体性しか持たないナヌークと、映画制作者によって女性らしさが増強されたナイラのような先住民がいることに気付くだけでなく、そこに不在なもの、つまり、画面に映し出されていないものがあることに注意を向けるようになる。「女性観客性」の実践とは、ナヌークに焦点が当てられている際にカメラにとらえられていないナイラは何をしているのかを、観客が考えることを意味する。このように、さまざまなメディアが作り出すメッセージを解読する際に批判的な視点を適用することにより、隠されているもの、つまり、語られないものがわかるのである。また、エンコーディングを批判的な視点から行うことにより、制作者は代替的な考え方を提案することができる。

7
エンコーディング第 1 工程：
アクティブ・ラーニングの導入

　前述のように、文科省は生徒たちの英語力涵養ならびに ICT 能力強化を重視している。また、最近は学校でアクティブ・ラーニングと呼ばれる教育方法を実践しようという動きがある。文科省は、高等教育を通じて「生涯を通じ学び、自分で考え、問題を調査し取り組むことができ、『生きる力』(zest for life) にもとづき、あらゆる状況に対応できる多様な人材の育成」(2013a) を目ざすという姿勢を打ち出している。その目的達成のために、文科省は「大学教育に関しては、アクティブ・ラーニング（生徒が問題および解決法を能動的に見つけ出す学習）、双方向の講義、演習、実験など、教育の質を変えるための種々の活動（activities）を促すべきである」(2013a) として、アクティブ・ラーニングを推奨している。このように、文科省はアクティブ・ラーニングが今後の教育に欠かせない学習活動の一つであると唱えている。

　日本とは異なり、北米の学校ではアクティブ・ラーニングがかなり以前から実践されている。また、その効果を調査するため、多くの研究が行われてきた（Barkley, 2010; Bean, 2011; Meyers & Jones, 1993; Prince, 2004）。文献調査にもとづき、Prince (2004) は、アクティブ・ラーニングの定義は研究者や学問分野によってさまざまであるとしながら、「アクティブ・ラーニングの中核となる要素は、学生の活動（activity）および学習過程での能動的な取り組み（engagement）である」(2004, p.223) という、多様な概念における共通点を指摘した。

　アクティブ・ラーニングのさまざまな定義がある中で、筆者は Barkley

の「アクティブ・ラーニングとは、能動的に参加する過程を通じて、自分自身で考え、概念、あるいは問題解決策を生み出し、その学びの過程を吸収し理解につなげることにより、生徒が知力を構築することを意味する」（2010, p.25）という定義が有用であると考える。このようなアクティブ・ラーニングが実践された場合、クラスはどのようなものになるのだろうか。Meyers & Jones（1993）は、アクティブ・ラーニングによる学習過程の劇的な変化を以下のように描写している。

> アクティブ・ラーニングが実践されたクラスでは、教師が教室の前から権力を行使し、主として講義を通じた知識の送信に依存することで生徒の学習を統制することはもはやない。その代わりとして、生徒が自身の学習に責任を持てるよう、教師はクラス内で生じることを監督し演出する。（p.56）

このようなアクティブ・ラーニングは、銀行型（つめこみ）教育を起源とする伝統的な指導法とは正反対である。Freire（2003）は、銀行型教育体制では「生徒たちは貯蔵所であり、教師は預金者である。コミュニケーションの代わりとして、教師はコミュニケ（声明）を出し、預金し、それを生徒たちが根気よく受け取り、暗記し、復唱する」（p.72）と説明している。この教師と生徒の不均衡な関係を改善するために、アクティブ・ラーニングが必要となる。アクティブ・ラーニングをクラスで確実に実行するには、教師が柔軟になり、生徒たちの自主性を促すファシリテーターの役割を果たす必要がある。

　本書で例示するフィルム－イング実践は、筆者が担当した授業で取り入れたアクティブ・ラーニングにもとづいている。ここで、筆者の担当したメディアに関する授業に触れ、そこでのアクティブ・ラーニングの実施について詳細に説明してゆきたい。当授業の目的は、メディアの特質およびメディアが生み出す表象を多角的な視点から捉えることにあった。受講者は、グローバルコミュニケーションに必要なクリティカル・メディアリテ

ラシーに重点を置き、授業やミュージアム、コミュニティーなどのさまざまな場面でクリティカル・メディアリテラシーを適用することの意義を探る。さらに、受講者は、メディア制作者と被写体、視聴者間に存在する社会的・文化的・政治的な関係性について考察する。この授業を通して、受講者はメディアリテラシーの概念についての理解を深め、メディアによって構築される多種多様なメッセージを認識・分析することができるようになる。授業計画は以下の通りである。

  1回目： オリエンテーション：グローバルコミュニケーションのための新たなリテラシー
  2回目： 日常のなかのさまざまなメディア
  3回目： 伝達形態（1）：新聞
  4回目： 伝達形態（2）：テレビとインターネット
  5回目： 反応形態
  6回目： ジェンダーの表象
  7回目： 人種、民族の表象
  8回目： 視線と権力
  9回目： メディアにおける倫理
  10回目： 21世紀のメディアの可能性
  11回目： 社会正義に向けてのメディア表現
  12回目： グローバルコミュニケーションに向けてのメディア表現
  13回目： 口頭発表（1）：メディアによる表象分析
  14回目： 口頭発表（2）：クリティカル・メディアリテラシーの応用
  15回目： まとめ

筆者はこの授業を2015年9月から2016年2月にかけて行った。受講者は、各回の授業で指定されたテキストで予習して、ディスカッションやグループ・ワーク、プレゼンテーションなどの活動に取り組んだ。

　授業の初期の段階では、多種多様なメディアおよびメディアリテラシーの概念の理解に重点を置いた。その後、新聞記事の構成など、メディアのメッセージを分析するための批判的思考を啓発した。さらに、メディアが

生み出すジェンダー、人種、民族に関するさまざまな表象（テレビコマーシャル、ミュージックビデオ、雑誌広告など）を分析することにより、クリティカル・メディアリテラシーの修得を促した。各自で分析をした後、学生は数人のグループを構成し、分析からわかったことについて話し合った。各グループから1名が代表して、この話し合いの過程と結果をクラス全体に発表した。Bean (2011) は、この種の活動は、「アクティブ・ラーニングおよび批判的思考の助長 ［中略］ ならびに専攻分野における探求者および研究者としての学生の成長促進」(p.149) に有益だとしている。

　こうした一連のディスカッションにより、受講者間により密接な関係が構築された。その結果、さらに活発な意見交換が促され、異なる価値観を尊重し合う友好的な環境が生まれた。このように、アクティブ・ラーニングがもたらす恩恵の一つは、「クラス内の学習コミュニティーの構築」(Barkley, 2010, p.27) である。Barkley (2010) は、高等教育において教師は「自分が学習コミュニティーの中に含まれ、尊敬され、重要であり、貢献している一員であるとすべての生徒が思えるよう手助けすること」(p.27) に鋭意努力すべきであるとしている。

　Meyers & Jones (1993) は、クラスにおける「学習コミュニティー」の確立がもたらす恩恵と、アクティブ・ラーニング強化に必要な次のステップについて述べている。

> 会話し、お互いの言うことに耳を傾けつつ、少人数のグループ・ディスカッションにおいて熟考することにより、生徒は自身の考えを明確にし、他の生徒の考えを尊重できるようになる。そして、少人数のグループに参加するための技能が修得できたら、生徒と教師は、さらにやりがいのあるアクティブ・ラーニングの形態——学生協働プロジェクト——に進む準備が整ったことになる。(p.73)

筆者の授業では、協力的な学習環境が確保された後、受講者にグループ・プロジェクトが課された。このプロジェクトは、撮影計画の作成およびクラスでの発表を目的とするものであった。日本を訪れる外国人観光客の数

が年々増加している（Naito, 2016）ことを踏まえ、より多くの観光客の興味を引くようにテレビコマーシャルを英語で制作する計画の立案が受講者に課された。ここからがフィルム－イング実践であり、Meyers & Jones (1993) が述べているところの「学生協働プロジェクト」である。本書のフィルム－イング実践は、このユニットで説明したアクティブ・ラーニングと切り離すことはできない。フィルム－イング実践にはいくつかの工程があるが、それについては次のユニットで説明する。

8
エンコーディング第2工程：
撮影技術の習得

　このユニットでは有用な撮影技術について述べる。手にカメラを持ち撮影する方法、三脚を使用した撮影方法、そしてカメラ動作（たとえばズーム、パン、ティルト）、カメラショット、アングル、照明、音響について説明する。これらの技術を身につけることで、映像作品を通して自身が伝えたいメッセージを効果的に発信することが可能となる。

ハンドヘルドと三脚使用

　まずは、手にカメラを持ち撮影する方法と、三脚を使用した撮影方法の2つをおさえておこう。ハンドヘルドとは、カメラを手に持ち、撮影することである（図1）。近距離の被写体をとらえたい場合、三脚よりも手にカメラを持ち撮影するのがよい。一方、カメラをできる限り安定させて撮影しなければならない場合もある。その際は、カメラを三脚に取り付けるのが有効である（図2）。ハンドヘルドによる撮影で被写体にズームインすると、画像がぐらついてしまう。視聴者を考慮し、不安定な画像は避けることが望ましく、三脚を使用することでこの問題は解消される。

ズーミング

　ズーミングは、よく知られている撮影技術の一つであるが、特別な理由がない限り、頻繁に使用するのは好ましくない。ズームインは、被写体に焦点を当てるものであり、逆に、ズームアウトは、被写体を取り巻く背景についての情報を提供する。ズームイン、ズームアウトとも多用するのは

避けるべきである。急速にズームインまたはズームアウトすると、視聴者は目が回ってしまうことにも注意しなくてはならない。ズーミングはスポーツ試合の撮影などには便利な撮影技術である。視聴者の注意を特定の選手に向けたい場合、その選手にズームインするのは理にかなっている。また、ドラマの撮影で、緊張が高まった雰囲気を表現するのにも効果的である。そうすることで、スリリングな場面を作り出すことができる。

パンニング

パンニングとはカメラを水平に動かす撮影技術のことである。この技術は視聴者にパノラマ風景を見せたり、動く被写体を捉えたりするのに最適である。たとえば、海の広大さを強調したり、見通しのよい場所で歩行あるいは走行している人を捉えたりするのに有用な撮影技術である。ただし、特別な理由がない限り、パンニングはしないのが望ましい。

ティルティング

ティルティングとはカメラを垂直に動かす撮影技術のことである。これは視聴者に高さのある被写体を見せるのに有効な撮影技術である。たとえば、スカイツリーや東京タワーなどの高層建築物を撮影する際、カメラを建築物の下部から上部へ、あるいは、上部から下部へ動かしながら撮影すると、建物の高さが強調されて効果的である。ズーミングやパンニングと同様、特別な理由があればティルティングを使用するとよい。

カメラショットの種類

ここでは、4種類のカメラショット（ワイド、ミディアム、クローズアップ、エキストリーム・クローズアップ）を覚えておくことが重要である。ワイド・ショット（WS）では、広々とした描写が可能となる。ワイド・ショットは、映画のストーリーのコンテクストを確立し、視聴者に対して、設定場所、登場人物、出来事を明らかにする。そのため、場面設定ショットとも呼ばれる。

ミディアム・ショット（MS）は、ワイド・ショットに比べると、限定されるが、より詳細な光景を映し出す。視聴者は被写体に注意を向けることができる（図9参照）。概して、ミディアム・ショットの中の登場人物は、ウェストから上の部分が映っている。

クローズアップ・ショット（CS）では、被写体が画面中心に位置する。視聴者は、このショットの被写体の表情を通して、反応（がっかり、ショック、驚きなど）や感情（怒り、嬉しさ、悲しみなど）を読みとることができる。

エキストリーム・クローズアップ・ショット（ECS）は、被写体のある一部にフォーカスしたものである。たとえば、目・口・手など被写体の体の一部分のみを映し出す。この撮影技術は主にアイシャドウや口紅などの化粧品の宣伝に使用される。

加えて、ツーショット（TS）と呼ばれ、ドキュメンタリー作品のインタビューでよく使われるものもある。このショットでは、画面の中に2人の人物を含み、たいていは質問者の肩越しに撮影し、インタビューに答える人物に焦点を当てている。

アングル

色々なアングルから撮影することで、多様性が生まれ、さまざまなメッセージを伝えることが可能となる。たとえば、上から撮影すると、被写体は弱々しく見えることがある。一方、下から撮影すると、被写体は堂々としており強く見える。図14からわかるように、上からのカメラ撮影では、視聴者は広々と開けた土地を見ることができる。図15から、下からのカメラ撮影は、被写体の高さや長さを強調する効果があることがわかる。

本書は、ここで挙げたカメラのアングルやショットを積極的に使用しながら撮影することを推奨する。自分にとって重要な人や物を撮影する場合、同じシーンをさまざまなアングルとショットを使って録画するとよい。この多様性がコンピューター上で映像編集を始めた際に多くの選択肢を与えてくれることになる。

照明

　カメラを使って撮影する際には、十分な光を確保しつつ、光源やその効果について考える必要がある。逆光で被写体を撮影するのは好ましくない。そうした場合は、被写体が暗くなりよく見えなくなってしまう。照明にはハードライトとソフトライトの2種類があることを理解しよう。Pogue（2006）は、「ハードライトは、対象に直接当たっている小規模な光源から来るものである。［中略］たとえば、直射日光のもとで誰か立っているとすると、その人の顔にできる影ははっきりしていて濃い」（pp. 48–49、強調は原文）と説明している。逆にソフトライトは、「間接的で、最も明るい部分から最も暗い部分にかけての光のグラデーションがより柔らかく、なめらか」（Pogue, 2006, p.49）である。これは別名「拡散光」と呼ばれ、「曇りの日の外光、あるいは、カメラマンが使用するアンブレラの反射光」（Pogue, 2006, p.49）と同様である。

　さらに、映像撮影には、一般的にキーライト、フィルライト、バックライトという3種類の光源が関係していることを知っておこう。Pogue（2006）は、それぞれの光源の特徴について次のように述べている。

> キーライトは、そのシーンにおける第一の光源を指す。たとえば、カメラ付属のライト、太陽の光、頭上から照らす光、あるいは、窓からの光のことである。［中略］フィルライトは、第二の光源である。［中略］室内照明等のキーライトによってできた影をやわらげる。［中略］バックライトは、被写体の背後から来る光のことである。被写体が背景に埋もれないようにしてくれる。（pp.49–50、強調は原文）

撮影する際、以上のことを頭に入れておけば、劇的な変化が期待できる。

音響

　カメラを使い記録する際には、音響の重要性を軽視してはならない。Millerson（2001）は、「最も価値のあるテレビ番組や映画作品を分析すると、情報を提供し視聴者のイマジネーションを刺激しているのは音響であ

ることに気付くことが多々あるだろう」(p.101、強調は原文）と述べている。このように、音響／音声は、映像撮影において重要な役割を果たしている。はっきりした音響／音声をとらえたい場合は、被写体の近くにカメラを置くことが必要となる。ブームマイクの使用が理想であるが、授業での使用となると、マイクをカメラに取り付けるのがよいだろう。あるいは、ボイスレコーダーで音響／音声を記録し、編集時にコンピューター上の編集ソフトに取り込むという方法もある。インタビューでは、はっきりした音声を確保することが重要である。万が一、記録した音声が聞きにくい場合は、編集段階で音量をある程度まで引き上げることも可能ではある（ユニット10参照）。

9
エンコーディング第3工程：
絵コンテ作成

　絵コンテとは、撮影前の準備として、映画制作者の考えや撮影計画を記録する図表のことである。絵コンテ作成により、映画制作プロジェクトの立案や推敲がしやすくなる。Millerson & Owens (2009) は、絵コンテ作成の効果について以下のようにまとめている。

> 　絵コンテにより下絵を描くことで、ディレクターは撮影の際のカメラの動きをイメージし、計画を立てるのが容易になる。各シーン、あるいは、まとまりのある一連のシーンでメインとなる場面をディレクターがどのように配列しようとしているのかを示す図表なのである。(p.86)

　絵コンテには撮影番号、アングル（上から、下からなど）、カメラショットの種類（ワイド、ミディアム、クローズアップ、エキストリーム・クローズアップ）、撮影時間、動作や会話についての描写などの重要な情報が書き込まれる。よって、絵コンテがあれば、映画制作者が視聴者に何を見せたいのかがわかりやすい。逆に、映画制作者側からすれば、絵コンテを作成するときには、頭に浮かぶイメージを絵に表現することが求められる。ただし、Millerson & Owens (2009) によると、覚えておくべき重要なことは、映画制作者が「よい絵コンテを作成するのに、絵がうまく描けないといけないということはない」(p.87) ということである。

　絵コンテ作成は撮影開始前の準備段階である。Millerson (2001) は、絵コンテ作成の効果について、「ある1シーンが次のシーンにどのようにつながるのかを考え始めるようになる。［中略］これにより、まとまりのあ

る一連の映像をもとに考える習慣が身につくであろう」(p.192)と指摘する。しかし、絵コンテで描いた絵の順番に従って撮影する必要はない。コンピューターを使用した編集で順番は簡単に変えられる。本書では、さまざまな授業で使用できるようにオリジナルの絵コンテを用意した（図16）。絵コンテはビジュアル、ボイスオーバー、サウンド／ミュージックの3つの欄で構成されている。ビジュアルの欄には、被写体とその動きを示すイラストを描く。ボイスオーバーとは、ナレーションのことであり、ナレーターのセリフや画面に映し出す言葉を書く欄である。サウンド／ミュージックの欄には、使用する効果音や音楽を記入する。ユニット11で挙げた、実際に学生が仕上げた絵コンテを参考にされたい。いずれにせよ、映画撮影を開始する前には絵コンテを作成し、計画を練っておくことを推奨する。

10
エンコーディング第4工程：
映像撮影と編集

　エンコーディングの最終工程として、映像撮影と編集について述べる。いよいよ作成した絵コンテをもとにカメラで撮影し、ユニット8で紹介した撮影技術を実践する時間である。撮影するときはいつも被写体に焦点が当たっていることを確認しよう。ズーミング、パンニング、ティルティングなどの撮影技術は、あまり速すぎずゆっくりと行わなくてはならない。したがって、実際に撮影する前にカメラ動作を練習しておくことを推奨する。前に述べたように、同じシーンをさまざまなアングルとショットを使って録画することが重要である。また、ズーミング、パンニング、ティルティングの前後では、少なくとも5秒間、カメラを安定させたまま録画をしておくことだ。これによって、編集段階でトランジション（場面変化）を加えるための十分なスペースが確保できる。編集に進む前に、記録した映像をカメラで直接再生したり、メモリーカード／スティックを用いてテレビやコンピューターで再生したりするなど、さまざまな方法で再生し確認するとよい。

　撮影が終了したら、編集の段階に進む。この段階では、動画編集ソフトウェアを利用し、映像や音声／音などの記録されたデータを編集する。これはノンリニア編集と呼ばれ、記録されたさまざまな映像や音声／音を結合させるものである。本書では、「Final Cut Pro」というソフトウェアを使用してノンリニア編集を行った。よく知られている動画編集ソフトウェアとしては、「i-Movie」や「Windows Movie Maker」がある。これらの動画編集ソフトウェアを使うことで編集が可能である。「Final Cut Pro」

を使用すると、映像や音声／音の長さを変えるためにクリップの長さを切る／調整することができるほか、シーンから次のシーンへの移行をスムーズにするためにトランジションを挿入したり、音声／音の大きさを調整したり、画面に文字を入れたり、透過度を変更することで複数のクリップを重ね合わせることができるなど、さまざまな編集が可能である。これらの動画編集ソフトウェアの使用方法については、すでに多くの手引書が出版されているため、本書では詳しく述べない。ただ、一つ覚えておくべきことは、記録されたデータの編集方法は人それぞれに異なり、我々が編集する際に行う選択は、自身が置かれている立場や価値観に影響を受けているということである。

　映像制作は理想的な表現方法になり得るが、撮影にあたっては倫理的側面を考慮する必要がある。撮影の被写体には事前に撮影について知らせておかなければならない。撮影の意図（何を撮影したいのか、何のために撮影するのか）を説明し、撮影に快く協力するかどうかについて被写体の意向を確認することがきわめて重要である。被写体が参加することに同意した場合のみ、撮影を開始することができる。被写体の同意については、書面で受け取ることを強く推奨する。そのためには、被写体が署名できるようにしかるべき同意書を準備する必要がある。映画制作者として、我々には被写体の疑問に答え、懸念に対応し、映画プロジェクト参加への正式な承諾を得る責任がある。

　なぜ被写体の同意を得ることが重要なのだろうか。我々が制作する映画は、被写体を描写し、エンコーディングの段階において、被写体について一定の表象（メッセージ）を作り出す。ユニット6で論じたように、映画制作（撮影と編集）に携わる際は、批判的な視点を持つことが必要不可欠である。映画制作者として、我々にはある特定の価値観を作品の中に挿入する力があることを理解しておこう。Kindon (2003) は、「これからの課題は、映像の取り扱い方に関与している権力についてもっと明らかにすること、多様な見解も部分的な見解も包含し民主的に映像を使用すること、そして知識に新しい可能性をもたらすことである」(p.149) と述べている。

映像制作では、言葉で、そして視覚的に、新しい考え方を提唱することができるが、我々が作り出す表象が被写体に関する固定観念的なイメージや偏見を再生産してしまう危険性がそこにはある。Dyer (1993) は、「……ステレオタイプは、現実について特定の定義と評価を表しており、それは社会における権力配置に関連している」(p.14) と指摘する。とすれば、映画制作者はどのようにして、ステレオタイプの再生産を回避することができるのだろうか。

このような問題に取り組むために、映画制作者は被写体のアイデンティティーの複雑さ、流動性、多様性に注目することが必要となる。Trinh (1991) は、以下の点を重視している。

> 人生で我々が経験することは、複雑で多様で不確実性に満ちあふれている。そして、この複雑さは、既成の解答による厳格な枠組みや映画の慣習の中におさめることはできない。人生を構成するものや被写体の内面のエネルギーのモンタージュおよび再現として、映像は、人生における経験の雑多性を組み入れる必要があるだろう。(p.112)

人々の多様性を映像制作に反映させようとするとき、インターセクショナリティー（交差性）という概念が役に立つ。Loutzenheiser (2005) は、「たとえば、人種、ジェンダー、階級、セクシュアリティー間の複雑なつながりを示す概念および明確な表現としてのインターセクショナリティーは、大きな可能性を秘めている」(p.27) と述べ、インターセクショナリティーという概念は、21世紀を生きる我々にとって必要不可欠だと主張している。映画制作者は、被写体のアイデンティティーを構築する多層の要素を認識し、被写体を単純・単一のカテゴリーに当てはめないようにする必要がある。

11
フィルム–イング実践

　ここでは、ユニット7で紹介したグループ・プロジェクトの開始とその展開について説明する。フィルム–イング実践を成功させるには、これまで見てきたように、学生たちが通過すべきいくつかの工程がある。具体的には、批判的思考力および撮影技術を修得し、絵コンテ作成と映像撮影、編集の方法について学び、最終的には英語を使いつつ、ある種の視覚的表現を生み出すことである。筆者の授業で実施されたフィルム–イング実践は、Freire (2003) の次の言葉の影響を受けている。

　　探究から離れ、実践から離れる場合、人は真に人間にはなれない。知識というものは、発明および再発明を通して、人間がこの世の中で、世界とともに、そして、人々が一緒に追い求めるような、休むことなく活力に満ち、継続して希望に満ちた探究を通してのみ現れる。(p.72)

Freire はこのように探究と実践は、教育に必須の要素であると主張している。本ユニットでは、フィルム–イング実践がいかにこれら2つの重要な要素を涵養するかを示し、それによっていかに指導と学びの環境が活気に満ちたものになるかを明らかにする。

実践の開始

　ユニット7ですでに論じたように、本書で例示するグループ・プロジェクトの目的は、外国人観光客が日本を訪れたいと思うようなテレビコマーシャルを立案し、発表することである。この授業の履修者数は31名で、学生たちは自発的に2〜5人のグループを形成した（図17）。プロジェク

トのために結成されたグループは、ディスカッションを重ねたグループと同じであった。これは非常に効果的である。なぜなら、毎週、さまざまなトピックについて同じメンバーで話し合うことは、「生徒の相互作用および友情を促進し、生徒たちの統率力を伸ばす助けとなり、多様性を助長する」(Bean, 2011, p.201) からである。フィルム－イング実践のために結成されたグループでは、メンバー同士が簡単に連絡を取れるよう、学生たちの間でもっともポピュラーな SNS の 1 つを使い連絡先を交換した。また、各グループは、メンバーをまとめるプロジェクトマネジャーを指名し、テレビコマーシャルのための制作会社名を決定した。

実践の展開

　講義とディスカッションを通じて、学習者はエンコーディングとデコーディングの関係や、世界中でさまざまなメディアにより生成され流通される多様なメッセージ等、メディアに関する知識を修得した。メディアによるメッセージの受信者としてデコーディングを行うのとは違い、フィルム－イング実践は生徒たちがエンコーディングを行う、換言すれば、自分たちでテレビコマーシャルを計画することでメッセージの発信者になることを可能にする。テレビコマーシャルの対象となる視聴者は海外の人々であり、コマーシャルに込めるのは、「旅に出て日本を探索しよう」というメッセージである。各グループは、記入するための絵コンテ用紙を受け取った。履修者全員が絵コンテ作成を今回初めて行うため、絵コンテの目的と記入すべき事項について説明し、イメージ図を描くこと、そして、ボイスオーバー／ナレーションとサウンド／ミュージックを具体的に書くことの意義を強調した（絵コンテについてはユニット 9 参照）。特にイメージ図の作成に備えて、カメラ動作、さまざまなカメラショットやアングルなどの撮影技術を指導するため、カメラ・ワークショップを実施した（ユニット 8 参照）。これは、学生たちが絵コンテを作成する際、各シーンに適切なカメラワークは何かを話し合い決定するのに役立った。

　これらの技術および知識を修得したところで、全グループに向けて次の

問いを提示した。

- ストーリー：どのようなストーリーを視聴者に伝えたいのか
- 人物：誰／何がコマーシャルに登場するのか
- ナレーション：ナレーションとして誰かの声を使用するのか、あるいは、画面に文字を載せるのか
- ミュージック／サウンド：どのようなミュージック／サウンドが好適かつ効果的であるか

各グループはブレインストーミングを行い、上記の問いをもとに意見を交換した（図18）。活発な話し合いの後にメンバー全員の考えをまとめ、グループでコマーシャルのテーマを決定した。

絵コンテ作成

それぞれのテーマを決定した後、すべてのグループが絵コンテの作成を開始した。最初に、各シーンのイメージ図を順に作り始めた（図19）。生徒たちはシーンの順番について熟考し、各シーンに合ったカメラワーク、ナレーション、ミュージック／サウンドについてグループメンバーと話し合った（図20）。プレゼンテーションの際に聴衆がコマーシャルをよりよく理解できるよう、グループの多くは絵コンテに色ペンや色鉛筆を使用した（図21）。英語でナレーションを制作するのが難しい生徒もいたため、筆者（教員）が各グループに生徒たちが伝えたいことを確認しつつ、日本語から英語にするサポートを行った。プレゼンテーションに先立って、すべてのグループのナレーション部分を筆者が校正・確認し、絵コンテはついに完成した（図22、図23参照）。

プレゼンテーション

プレゼンテーションに備えて、各グループは誰がどの部分を発表するのか分担を決め、英語のナレーションを担当する生徒たちは、教員とともに発音練習を行った。絵コンテの発表を行ったのは、合計で10グループで

あった。完成した絵コンテを観客に見えやすくするため、各グループは、デジタル映写システムに接続しているオーバーヘッドプロジェクター（OHP）を使用した（図24）。スマートフォンでミュージック／サウンドを再生しつつ、各グループはシーンのイメージ図を順を追って示し、ナレーションを音読した。その後、前述の問いにもとづき絵コンテを説明した。テーマについて説明し、ストーリーや登場人物、ナレーション、ミュージック／サウンドに関して、なぜそのような選択をしたのか説明した（図25）。グループが考案したテーマは、「日本の名所」「日本食」「日本の四季」「日本の花」「小旅行」「日本のカワイイ」「5レンジャーズと日本のイメージ」などである。グループが発表しているとき、観客のマナーはよく（図26）、他のグループのプレゼンテーションを熱心に聞き、発表が終わると発表者に拍手喝采した。生徒たちがこのようにお互いの話を敬意を表しつつ聞くような空間を、指導者が作り出すことが必要不可欠である。

実践の結果

ここではフィルム－イング実践の結果をまとめる。Palys（2003）が論じる「双方向的な」研究方法の特質と指針を参考にしながら、2016年2月1日にアンケート調査を実施した。生徒たちの意見を重視し、フィルム－イング実践を行った感想を把握するため、質問を選択形式と自由記述の両方で行った（表1）。

表1　アンケート調査質問例

選択形式： 絵コンテを作成するというグループ・プロジェクトはどうでしたか？（どれか1つに○） ・5　大変良い ・4　良い ・3　普通 ・2　あまり良くない

- 1 悪い

もしこの授業が通年（半期でなく1年間）だとしたら、自分たちの絵コンテをもとに映画を作ってみたいと思いますか？（どれか1つに○）
- 5 大変そう思う
- 4 そう思う
- 3 まあまあ思う
- 2 あまり思わない
- 1 思わない

自由記述：
授業で学んだ色々なカメラワークについてどう思いますか？
絵コンテを作った感想を書いてください。
グループ・プロジェクトを通してどのようなことを学びましたか？

　まず、生徒たちの次のような回答から、さまざまなカメラ動作やカメラショット、アングルについて指導を受けたカメラ・ワークショップが有益だったことが示された。

> K：「テレビコマーシャルやドラマなどのシーンをカメラワークの撮り方で見るようになった」
> H：「これらの撮影技術を自分で写真を撮るときの参考にしたい」
> Y.I：「学んだ撮影技術を今後使って動画を作ってみたい」

このように、撮影技術の指導により、マスメディアに対する新たな見方を持ったり、授業で学んだことを自身の日常生活に適用しようと考えたりする学生が現れたと考えられる。
　カメラ・ワークショップの後に開始した絵コンテに関しては、多くの学生が以下の2名と同様の意見を持っている。

> ハセ：「絵コンテを作ったのは初めてだったので、良い経験になった」
> グレイシア：「自分たちで絵を描いて、音楽も考えてとても大変だったけれど、楽しかった」

これらの言葉から、生徒の気持ちの中で楽しさと苦しさが混在していることが明らかである。同様の状況が、絵コンテの発表について述べたM.Kの「自分たちが伝えたいことを聞いてくれている人たちに伝える難しさやメンバーと1つのものを作る楽しさを感じた」という言葉に見てとれる。

アンケート調査への以下の回答は、多くの生徒が苦労しながらもさまざまな事柄を学び、グループ発表に肯定的であることを示している。

> マリー：「見ている人たちに自分たちのグループが伝えたいことを限られたスペースと時間で表現することが楽しかったです」
> RV：「発表の手順や進め方を学ぶことができた」
> ワキー：「それぞれのグループの英語の発音が良かった。絵が上手なので、絵コンテが見やすかった」

確かに多数の生徒がグループ・プロジェクトを行うことを好んでいる。それは以下の回答にもはっきりと現れている。

表2　グループ・プロジェクトに対する生徒たちの考え

絵コンテを作成するというグループ・プロジェクトはどうでしたか？（どれか1つに○）	n	%
5　大変良い	22	70.97
4　良い	7	22.58
3　普通	2	6.45
2　あまり良くない		
1　悪い		
合計	31	100.00

表 2 に見られるように、およそ 71 パーセントの生徒がグループ作業の経験に最高評価を付けた。

また、学生の多くがグループ・プロジェクトを通して協力することの大切さを学んだと回答した。チョンの「メンバーと協力して考えて行動する楽しさを感じた！」という言葉がグループ作業を支持する多数派の意見を代表している。しかし、ジャッキーの「友だちと話し合って作っていくことの難しさと楽しさを実感した」という言葉が示すように、協力することは容易ではない。一方で、その困難を乗り越え、豊かな学習体験を得ることができる学生もいる。スプリングの「協力してそれぞれの苦手なところを補ったりすることの大切さを学んだ」という言葉にあるように、協働学習は能動的な学習者としての生徒の意識を高めることができる。

このようなプラスの効果がある協働学習を実現するために、生徒は何をすべきかについて、Barkley (2010) は以下のように説明する。

> 真の学習コミュニティーになるのは、骨の折れる作業である。学生たちには、居心地のよい受身の状態から抜け出してリスクを冒し、新たな役割を担い、多くの大学の教室で使い慣れているものとは違う技能を伸ばすことが求められる。学生たちは意見の相違を認め、個々の違いを尊重することで、協力し衝突を解決する必要がある。(pp.125–126)

Barkley がここで述べていることをフィルム−イング実践に当てはめれば、生徒たちが居心地の良い場所から飛び出し、指導者がファシリテートする前向きで親密さのただよう空間において自己を表現し、他者の意見に耳を傾け始めたとき、「真の学習コミュニティー」が出現すると言える。このことは、ミンジーの「自分の意見ばかり主張するのでなく、みんなで考えを出し合って作った方が自分の考えていたものより良いものが作れた」という回答に裏付けされている。

さらに、アンケート調査結果は、フィルム−イング実践についてもう一つの興味深い点を示している。

表3　映画制作に対する生徒たちの考え

もしこの授業が通年（半期でなく1年間）だとしたら、自分たちの絵コンテをもとに映画を作ってみたいと思いますか？（どれか1つに○）	n	%
5　大変そう思う	9	29.03
4　そう思う	14	45.16
3　まあまあ思う	7	22.58
2　あまり思わない		
1　思わない	1	3.23
合計	31	100.00

　生徒の多くが授業で取り扱った内容をもとに映画を制作することに前向きな姿勢を持っていることが、回答から明らかである。この授業は9月から2月までの半期という時間の制限があるので、視覚的表現として絵コンテを完成させることが最終目標である。もしこの授業が通年であれば、完成した絵コンテにもとづいて撮影を行うことが可能になる。つまり、4月から8月の間、生徒たちはユニット6から10で示した教材をすべて学び、9月から翌年2月にかけて、撮影ならびに編集を行い、最後に映画を上映することができる。アンケート調査は、多くの生徒がフィルム－イング実践に好意的であることを示している。筆者は、指導者が柔軟性を持ち、各授業の目標・規模・期間・学生集団に適した実践を行うことが望ましいと考える。次のユニットでは、フィルム－イング実践の産物を紹介する。

12
映画脚本

『幽玄（Yugen）』
デジタルカラー映画4分
制作＝原紘子、Hara Pekkori Girls プロダクション
編集＝原紘子
公開＝2015年
撮影地＝日本
声＝サマンサ（声1）、ジャスミン（声2）、キャナコ（声3）、リサ（声4）
音楽＝「調和／不調和を越えて」原紘子（作）
リズム＝キャナコ、ジャスミン、リサ、サマンサ

声1：「西／東」
声2：「ここ／そこ」
声3：「中心／周縁」
声4：「出発点／終着点」

声1：
「西／東」
「日本人／非日本人」
「単一／複雑」

字幕：
すいすい
（Smooth）

ひらひら
　（Fluttering）

声2：
「ここ／そこ」
「現在／過去」
「身体／精神」

字幕：
ぷかぷか
　（Floating）

さらさら
　（Rustling）

声3：
「光／闇」
「中心／周縁」
「旧／新」

字幕：
ぴかぴか
　（Sparkling）

ゆらゆら
　（Wavering）

声4：
「内部者／外部者」
「目に見えるもの／目に見えないもの」
「出発点／終着点」

映画脚本

字幕：
ふわふわ
（Airy）

いきいき
（Full of life）

声1：
「西と東の境がにじむ」
「日本人と非日本人の境がにじむ」
「単一と複雑の境がにじむ」

声2：
「こことそこの境がにじむ」
「現在と過去の境がにじむ」
「身体と精神の境がにじむ」

声3：
「光と闇の境がにじむ」
「中心と周縁の境がにじむ」
「旧と新の境がにじむ」

声4：
「内部者と外部者の境がにじむ」
「目に見えるものと目に見えないものの境がにじむ」
「出発点と終着点の境がにじむ」

声1：
「西／東」
「日本人／非日本人」
「単一／複雑」

　　　　　　　字幕：
　　　　　　　すいすい
　　　　　　　　（Smooth）

　　　　　　　ひらひら
　　　　　　　　（Fluttering）

声 2：
「ここ／そこ」
「現在／過去」
「身体／精神」

　　　　　　　字幕：
　　　　　　　ぷかぷか
　　　　　　　　（Floating）

　　　　　　　さらさら
　　　　　　　　（Rustling）

　　　　　　　　　　　　　　　声 3：
　　　　　　　　　　　　　　　「光／闇」
　　　　　　　　　　　　　　　「中心／周縁」
　　　　　　　　　　　　　　　「旧／新」

　　　　　　　字幕：
　　　　　　　ぴかぴか
　　　　　　　　（Sparkling）

　　　　　　　ゆらゆら
　　　　　　　　（Wavering）

声 4 :
「内部者／外部者」
「目に見えるもの／目に見えないもの」
「出発点／終着点」
（声 1 から 4 が重なる）

     字幕 :
     ふわふわ
      （Airy）

     いきいき
     （Full of life）

声 1 :
「西と東の境がにじむ」
「日本人と非日本人の境がにじむ」
「単一と複雑の境がにじむ」

          声 2 :
         「こことそこの境がにじむ」
         「現在と過去の境がにじむ」
         「身体と精神の境がにじむ」

声 3 :
「光と闇の境がにじむ」
「中心と周縁の境がにじむ」
「旧と新の境がにじむ」

          声 4 :
         「内部者と外部者の境がにじむ」

「目に見えるものと目に見えないものの境がにじむ」
「出発点と終着点の境がにじむ」
（声1から4が重なる）

字幕：
「筆を手にしたあなたは、
何を表現しますか」

「表現するのは、あなたの番です」

13
映画プロジェクト事例研究

　また幽玄の物真似では、強さの理を忘れてはならない。
(Zeami, 2005, p.95)

　前ユニットでは、映画『幽玄』（2015年制作）の脚本と映画から抜粋された静止画を示した。この映画は、筆者の2年ゼミに所属する学生たちと共同で撮影・制作したものである。ゼミは小規模だが、通年科目であるため、学生たちにはフィルム－イング実践を行い、映画を完成させるのに十分な時間がある。したがって、この実践は、さまざまな規模の通年授業にとって有用な例を提供することができる。また、完成した映画は、学生たちがデコーディングとエンコーディングの能力および撮影技術を修得した後、自己の考えを言葉と視覚でどのように表現するのかを示す良い例であるといえる。この映画の概念的枠組みを構成する4つの主なポイントは、幽玄という概念、書道、ストーリーテリング、リズムである。このユニットでは、各ポイントについて詳細に説明する。

幽玄という概念
　筆者のゼミのメンバーであるキャナコ、ジャスミン、リサ、サマンサの4人の学生は、アメリカやオーストラリアでの留学経験があり、留学先の現地の人々に日本文化に関する質問をされたという共通点がある。そこで、日本文化に根付いた概念についての研究を行い、活発なディスカッションを通して、幽玄という概念を用いるのが自分たちの映画プロジェクトに適切だという結論に至った。能の大家である世阿弥が、能の理論と実践を通じて幽玄という概念を発展させたと言われている。世阿弥作『風姿花

伝』の翻訳者である Wilson（2006）は、幽玄の概念について次のように述べている。

> 日本の初期の詩（歌）の美学では、幽玄は「もののあはれ」の深遠で不可知でありながら、優雅な趣を意味した。後に幽玄は、優雅で名状しがたい美ならびに哀愁を伴った高雅な簡素および寛大さを意味するようになった。世阿弥はこれらすべての意味ならびにニュアンスを受け継ぎ、精通していた。(p.170)

日本文化はある種の繊細で深遠な特色を持っているが、それらを視覚化するには、幽玄の概念は「何かを完全に暴露するというよりむしろ暗示し、苦心して描写するというよりむしろ示唆し喚起することができる」（Trinh, 1991, p.162）ものであるため、理想的であるとゼミのメンバーたちの意見が一致した。

書道

映画制作チームは書道の重要性に注目した。サマンサが「日本の学校では小さいときから書道を学ぶ」と述べているように、書道は重要な文化的素養の一つである。上述の幽玄という概念を踏まえ、学生は映画の中で水墨画制作を実演することに決めた。その理由について、ジャスミンは、「書道は日本の伝統です。筆を使うことで、字だけではなくて絵も描けるということを伝えたい」と説明した。

Okamoto（2015）が「日本の水墨画は、簡素の伝統美を直感的表現の独特な強調と結びつける」（p.8）と指摘したように、幽玄の概念は、水墨画に大きな影響を及ぼしている。水墨画では墨の色に考慮することが重要である。Mayhall（1989）は、「ある混合物が黒、灰色の濃淡、白の中で出現し、……それがあらゆる色を示しうる」（p.9）と水墨画について述べている。加えて、映画の中でオオカミの水墨画を描いたキャナコは、「筆でオオカミを描いた。自分が表現したいものを色の濃さだけで表現できることは、日本文化のステキなところだと思う」と述べた。水墨画における灰色

の可能性について、Trinh（2013）は「この新しい色相は他とはまったく別な色であり、黒でも白でもなくどこか中間にあるもので、無限の可能性がある」(p.125)と述べた。

また、筆で字を書くということは単なる文字表記ではない。Reed（1989）は、「言葉で表しがたい概念の力を筆は増大させる。描くという動作は強烈で即時的であるが、持続的な跡、つまり、書を生み出した人の精神の躍動的な痕跡を残す」(p.23)と、芸術としての書の力について述べた。よって、映画制作チームは筆で絵を描き、筆・墨・紙の結合から生じる色を通して幽玄の概念を表現し、新たな観念や感覚を視聴者に喚起することを目ざした。

ストーリーテリング

概して、映画には視聴者に話をするナレーター（語り手）がいる。Trinh（2013）は著書の中で、映画におけるストーリーテリングに注目し、映画制作者にとって重要なのは、自己の立ち位置はどこか、どのように語るべきか、どの／だれの話を語るべきかをよく考えることだと述べている。映画制作チームは、灰色の概念の影響を受けた立場から語りかけることに決め、黒／白という二項対立を超越する新たな視点をもたらそうと志した。このような目的から、映画『幽玄』には、出発点／終着点、ここ／そこ、内部者／外部者、現在／過去などの英語の対義語を声に出して言う4人のストーリーテラーがいるのである（ユニット12参照）。

留学経験はゼミのメンバーに大きな影響を及ぼしている。たとえば、ジャスミンは、アメリカ留学を通じた自身の変化について次のように述べた。

> 1年生で初めて外国に行った！　母語以外を学ぶことはとても大変なことだと思った。でも、前よりも英語でコミュニケーションがスムーズにできるようになって、自分の成長を感じた。

アメリカでの自身の体験を振り返り、リサは「here/there、origin/destination、insider/outsider などのそれぞれの言葉が留学生活でのさまざまな国の人との出会いや関わりを表していると思う」と述べた。彼女が指摘するように、映画『幽玄』のストーリーテラーたちは、「こことそこの境がにじむ」「出発点と終着点の境がにじむ」「内部者と外部者の境がにじむ」「西と東の境がにじむ」など、相対する要素を融合させることに言及している。このように、学生たちは、自身の体験に密接に関連する言葉を発する声を録音した。

英語に加えて、映画制作チームは、自分たちが育った言語を探究することに決めた。ポストコロニアル研究の著名な人物である Ngũgĩ（1986）は、言語と文化の相互関係を明瞭に表現している。

> 言語は文化を伴い、文化は特に口承および文学を通じて、自己ならびに世界における自己の立場を知覚する価値体系を伴う。人々がどのように自己を知覚するかが文化、政治、富の社会的生産、自然やその他のものとの全体的な関係についての見方に影響を及ぼす。言語はこのように特有な形と性質、特有の歴史、世界との特有の結びつきを持つ人間の共同体として、我々から切り離すことはできない。(p.16)

Ngũgĩ の説を参考に、ゼミのメンバーは、ストーリーテリングの方法として日本語と英語、つまり、第一言語と第二言語の両方を用いることに決定した。

その後、映画制作チームは、日本語の印象的な点について話し合い、たくさんのオノマトペ（擬音語・擬態語）があることに気付いた。Fukuda（2003）によれば、オノマトペは日本文化に根づいている。

> これは全く小さなことではなく、オノマトペは、日本語の最も重要で、独特で、強烈な面の一つである。日本語のネイティブスピーカーにとって、オノマトペは単なる言葉ではなく、そこから世界を眺める、いわば窓なのである。これらの言葉は、日本人の人生に対する見方をかなりの程度まで示している。(p.9)

キャナコが「普段よく学校でオノマトペを使う」と言うように、確かにオノマトペは、ゼミのメンバーの日常生活に密接している。オノマトペに注目し、Millington（1993）は、「概して、彼らの言語は感覚を表現する言葉が豊富であり、英語は動作を表現する言葉が豊富である」（p.12）と述べ、いかに日本語が英語と異なるかを論じている。そして、日本語の特徴に関して、「日本人は、事物がどのように感じられるのかについてきわめて敏感であり、あるものの感触あるいは雰囲気を描写するためのオノマトペがたくさんある」（p.12）と説明した。サマンサが「オノマトペの豊富さを知ってほしい」と言うように、制作チームは、「すいすい」「ひらひら」「ぷかぷか」「さらさら」「ぴかぴか」「ゆらゆら」「ふわふわ」「いきいき」等のオノマトペを挙げ、映画の中に含めた。

リズム

ストーリーテリングに加えて、Trinh（1999）は「人が気付こうが気付くまいが、リズムが人の映画についての体験を特色づけ、今すぐにはっきりと表せないとしても、人に記憶させておくのである」（p.198）と述べ、映画の中ではリズムが重要な役割を果たすと指摘する。制作チームは、映画のためにリズムを創作することに重点を置いた。学生は拍子をとり、プラスチックのカップを使いリズムを刻んだ。そのような練習を重ねた後、演奏を記録した（図32）。学生が創作したリズムに従って、テンポが速くリズム演奏と合わせて完成形となる「調和／不調和を越えて」という曲を筆者が制作した。

加えて、言葉に包含されたリズムに注意を払う必要がある。ゼミメンバーは、英語のリズムおよび音について体験したことを語った。リサは、「留学を通して英語を使い、話をすることがより身近になり、声に出して発音することが楽しいと気付いたため、それを音楽に合わせて楽しく伝えたかった」と述べた。また、ジャスミンは、「自分は発音に気をつけた。日本人の苦手な 'r' と 'l' の違いと 'b' と 'v' の違いが難しい」と述べた。

以上のように、4人の学生は映画『幽玄』の基礎をなす概念的枠組みを

作り、撮影を行った。この映画プロジェクトで、筆者は作曲や編集、プロデューサーの役割を果たし、編集した映像について彼らと協議し、映画の中に残すものと残さないものについて確認し合った。相談した結果を反映させて映画を完成させ、2015年10月の学園祭で上映した。グループインタビューでは、以下のように、制作チームメンバー全員がフィルム－イング実践を行うことを勧めている。

> キャナコ：「英語を使うことで、逆に日本文化を考えなおすことができた。英語を使い映画を作ることを学生にお勧めします」
> サマンサ：「はい、お勧めします。なぜならば、英語でしかできない表現があるから」
> リサ：「強くお勧めします！音楽、言葉、日本文化を混ぜてメッセージ性のあるものができた」
> ジャスミン：「英語が好きな友人と1つのものを作ることは本当に楽しいと思う。リズムも自分たちで作れて良かった」

このように映画制作チームは映画『幽玄』を誇りとしている。メンバーと筆者は日本国内外の映画祭に本作を出品しようと努めている。

14
観客

> ただし、あくまでもこの道は観客を本とすることを心得るべきである。
> （Zeami, 2005, p.80）

　前述したように、Hall（1999）はマスメディアにおけるエンコーディングとデコーディングの複雑な関係について探究した（ユニット6参照）。Ellsworth（1997）は、この関係を映画学と教育学の視点から研究し、エンコーディングを「伝達」、デコーディングを「反応」と呼んだ。Ellsworthは、対象とする観客に向けてあるメッセージ／情報を伝える映画制作者の手法を「伝達モード」、観客が映画などからメッセージ／情報を得る方法を「反応モード」とした。

　Ellsworthの主張は、映画『幽玄』にも当てはまる。なぜなら、そこには伝達と反応の両方のモードが存在するからである。Ellsworthは、「一つの映画の中にあるさまざまな形式や表現方法には、種々の伝達モードが使われることがある。多数の伝達モードが同時に使われていることもある」（1997, p.27）と述べている。『幽玄』では、水墨画の深み、日本語のオノマトペによる表現の豊かさ、英語でコミュニケーションをとることに伴う喜びなど、制作チームメンバーが伝えたいと願う複数のメッセージを込めるために、複数の伝達モードが用いられている。

　Ellsworthが「映画には意図され想像された観客がいる。望まれる観客もいる」（1997, p. 23）と述べるように、制作チームは映画プロジェクトを展開する上でターゲットとする観客を想定した。具体的には、日本語と英語の両方を映画の中で用いて、英語を学習しているか留学経験がある、あるいはその両方の学生ならびに英語圏に住む人々に向けて上述のメッセ

ージを伝達することを意図した。「灰色」の立場から複数のストーリーを語りつつ、映画制作チームは観客が多様な解釈をすることを望んだ。こういった目的を達成するのに必要なものは何か、Trinh（1991）は次のように述べている。

> 耳と目の多様で活発な関係を引き出し、観客自身が声明あるいは連続する映像から何を理解したいかを決める余地をより多く残すには、固定されたものを揺るがすような大規模な方策を生み出すことが必要である。
> （p.206）

学生によって、留学して得るものや日本での学校生活を送る方法はさまざまである。したがって、制作チームは揺るがない唯一の信念を押し付けるのではなく、映画『幽玄』を通じて観客が自身の経験や生活様式について思いをめぐらすよう促している。

では、対象である観客は、映画についてどのような解釈を行うのだろうか。観客の反応モードは、映画制作者の意図するものと一致するのだろうか。これらの問いの答えを得るには、観客となった学生の話を聞き、映画をどのように解釈したのかを調べることが重要である。筆者の担当する1年ゼミ（2015年度）に所属するシャーロット、ジェシカ、カレン、リリー、ノエルの5人の学生は、アメリカでの留学経験を持つ。彼らはメディア研究に関する英語のテキストを講読し、ユニット5で詳述したクリティカル・メディアリテラシーを修得した。また、ゼミ活動として、映画『幽玄』を鑑賞し話し合った。映画に関するそれぞれの第一印象からディスカッションは始まった。

ノエル：「わからない。水墨画の意味は何なのだろう？　幽玄の意味は何なのだろう」
カレン：「私には難解すぎる。映画をまた見たい」
リリー：「なぜ対義語を使っているのか理解できない。私には難しい」
シャーロット：「最初は単語がたくさん出てきたので、言葉についての

映画だと思った。けれど、途中から絵を描く場面があった。この映画が何を伝えたいのか理解できない」
　ジェシカ：「私には難しいので、もう一度見たい」

　カレンとジェシカが提案し、彼らは映画を再度視聴し、理解しようと努力した。
　『幽玄』に含まれる多様な伝達モードを通じて、5名の学生は映画の中のさまざまな要素に注目した。英語の対義語を発音する方法がカレンにとって最も印象的だった一方、ジェシカとノエルは、水墨画に最も強い印象を受けたと述べた。シャーロットとリリーは、「境がにじむ（blurred）」という単語の使用が最も印象的だと述べた。これらの印象に加えて、彼らは映画に関するさまざまな疑問も挙げた。

　ジェシカ：「オノマトペはどのような目的で映されていたのか」
　リリー：「なぜオノマトペ、対義語、水墨画を選んだのか」
　ノエル：「なぜ絵を描いたのだろうか」
　シャーロット：「なぜ対義語やオノマトペが映画に出てくるのか」
　カレン：「誰かが何かを言うときに、別の人も話しだす。声が重なる。
　　　　　その理由は何なのだろうか」

　上記の疑問を投げかけつつ、彼らは映画の内容で難解で混乱させるような点について話し合った。そこで彼らに共通していたのは、映画の中の映像と文字、声の関係を理解するのが困難だったことである。観客はストーリーテラーたちが英語の対義語を発音する声を聞きつつ、スクリーンに水墨画のパフォーマンスおよび日本語のオノマトペの単語が映し出されるのを見る。映画のエンディングに向かって対義語を音読する方法が変化していく。初めはストーリーテラーが一人ずつ単語を発音する。その後、ストーリーテラーたちの音読する声が重なり、そこで声の層が生じる。映画はこの工程を繰り返し、それにより観客を困惑させる。Trinh（1991）の「たとえば、一つの文をいろいろな部分で切り離し、間をおき組み立て、少し違

った形式、そして絶えず変化する口頭および視覚コンテクストで繰り返すことは、意味の不断の変化ならびに不安定を生じさせる助けとなる」（p.206）という分析がこの場合にあてはまる。映画『幽玄』もそのような機能を持つと考えて良いだろう。

　観客が感じたと指摘する困難や混乱は自然な反応である。Ellsworth (1997) は、映画制作者と視聴者の伝達および反応の関係を詳しく述べる。

> 映画の伝達モードが知識、ジェンダー、人種、セクシュアリティーにおいて不変の首尾一貫した立場、つまりその映画が解釈される<u>べき位置を</u>いくら構築しようとしても、実際の視聴者は、そのような伝達モードに反する映画の解釈を常に行い、映画が語りかけるところとは異なる位置から映画に<u>答えてきた</u>。（p.31、強調は原文）

このように Ellsworth は、映画制作者の伝達モードと観客の反応モードは必ずしも一致しないと指摘する。同様に、教室で上映する映像を生徒たちがどのように見るのかについて注目し、Miller & Zhou (2007) は、「視聴者は多種多様なフィルター（見方）を持ち込む」（p.332）と説明した。Ellsworth によると、不一致／矛盾は除去すべきでないという。確かに、映画制作者と観客の一方的でない相互的な関係を作るには、緊張は避けられない。Trinh (1991) はこのような相互関係を「相互学習」とみなし、「映画の制作者と被写体、観客の間には持ちつ持たれつの強い関係があり、映画の解釈を、映画制作者の意図だけに要約することは決してできない」（p.109）としている。

　Trinh が述べるように、映画『幽玄』も多様な解釈の仕方が可能である。それは以下に挙げた 5 人の観客である学生たちのコメントからも明らかである。

> カレン：「映画には日本独特のオノマトペが出てきた。同じようにアメリカ特有のものもたくさんある。たとえば、サンクスギビングなどの特別な行事がある。アメリカで勉強していたとき、そのような行事を

初めて体験した」
シャーロット：「日本では、文字を書いたり絵を描くほかにも言葉に表さないで伝えるという伝達方法がある。映画を見て、人の気持ちを察するなどの非言語コミュニケーションについて考えた。一方、アメリカでは考えを言葉に出すということが最も大事なことのように私は感じた」
ジェシカ：「この映画には対義語がたくさん含まれている。2つの対極するものが合わさって新しいものを生み出すと思う」
ノエル：「この映画は、カリフォルニアでの学生生活を思い出させる。そこでは、さまざまな国の人々と触れ合うことで、偏見をなくしたり、視野を広げたりすることができた。偏見をなくすには、いろいろな文化がお互いに触れ合う場所に身を置くことが大切」
リリー：「反対を作り出している考え方を見直し、すべてを合わせて考えることが必要だというメッセージを映画から受け取った」

以上の談話より、観客である学生一人一人が映画を違ったふうに解釈したのは明らかである。Trinh（1991）は、凝り固まったメッセージを押し付けずに、豊かな想像力を養成する映画について次のように述べている。

> 映画を解釈することは創造的な行為であり、解釈を統制するのでなく、喚起し伝えられるような映画を私は作り続けるだろう。映画というのは、私が視聴者に提供する一枚の用紙のようなものである。用紙の境界内にあるものは私に責任があるが、その折り重ねについては統制せず、統制しようとも思わない。視聴者がそれを水平に、斜めに、垂直に折り重ねることができ、成分を自身の好みやバックグラウンド（背景）に織り込むことができる。このような相互に折り重ね、相互に見る状況が映画制作において私は最も刺激的だと考える。(p.109)

このように、映像制作者にとって非常に重要なのは、自身と観客の複雑な関係に注意を向け、観客による多様な反応と解釈を認めることである。

15
結論

　私にとって、美術による表現も文字による表現も、根本的には同じものである。新しい精神の領域を開拓していく方法として、どちらも存在しているのである。そして、いずれにおいても、私は常に前衛であることを目指している。（草間、2012, p.236）

　我々の日常生活に視覚文化と技術が与える影響を軽視することはもはやできない。授業での指導と学習は、写真撮影やビデオ撮影、SNSを通じた共有という現代社会の風潮と切り離して行うことはできない。若い世代の人々がグローバル化とデジタル化が進む世界に能動的に参加できるようにするために、教育も進歩する必要がある。本書では、若い人々が熱心な学習者になり、それによって活気に満ちた地球市民になるよう促す上で、アートが重大な役割を果たすことを示してきた。

　研究者たちは、教育の分野にアートを統合することの利点を指摘してきた（Goldberg, 2001; Goodlad & Morrison, 1980; Shohat & Stam, 1994）。たとえば、Goodlad & Morrison（1980）は次のように述べている。

　　アートの教育学上の良さは、適切に考えられ教えられた場合、学習者側に無限の自己関与を与えてくれることである。［中略］未知の経験をもたらす体験およびこれらの体験に関するとどまることのない解釈は、目的ならびに手段を同時に与えてくれる。（p.11）

このようにGoodlad & Morrisonは、教育においてアートを用いることで、学習者に良い影響があると指摘している。
　Goldberg（2001）も学校教育にプラスの変化をもたらすアートの力につ

いて以下のように述べている。

> アートは、学習のための方法論あるいは戦略として、伝統的な指導法をあるテーマの探究に向けた大変ワクワクするような想像力に富むものへと拡大するのに役立つのである。クラスにおいてアートを教具として用いることは、アート<u>について</u>教えるという、より因習的な方法からその機能を広げ、生徒たちが理解を変化させ、自分たちの考えを独創的な形で応用する機会を与える。（p.25、強調は原文）

ここで Goldberg は、カリキュラムでアートを用いることにより指導と学習の新たな形態が生まれると主張している。さらに、「表現言語としてアートは、クラスの中のさまざまな声を起こすもとになり、すべての生徒が知識と連携するための多くの道を切り開く」（p.25）と述べ、教育現場においてアートを活用すれば、意見を述べたり、知識構築に取り組んだりするのに多様な方法が可能になると主張している。

このような流れの中で、学者たちはアートベースの教育と研究には多くの可能性があることを証明してきた（Barone & Eisner, 2012; Eisner, 2002; Hickman, 2007; Leavy, 2015; Siegesmund & Cahnmann-Taylor, 2008）。たとえば、Siegesmund & Cahnmann-Taylor（2008）は、アートを教育現場や教育的研究に活用することで生まれる可能性について、次のように論じている。

> アートベースの教育的研究は、特に学習を高める人間関係を理解し啓蒙するのに非常にふさわしいものである。そのような研究は、すぐれた指導がいかに生徒を深い学習の構造に引き込むかを理解するのに役立つ証拠を提供することができる。そのような学習成果は個人の自主性であり、換言すれば、自身のストーリーを表す勇気を持つことにより、自分自身の人生を想像力豊かに形成する能力を持った自主的な個人である。
>
> (p.244)

このように、Siegesmund & Cahnmann-Taylor は、芸術的な探究と実践が学びの質を高めるだけでなく、表現や創作における生徒たちの自主性を育成する強力な手段として機能するとしている。

　本書で紹介したフィルム－イング実践には、以上のようなプラスの特色がある。筆者が以前論じたように（Hara, 2016 参照）、映像制作は、教育におけるアートベース・アプローチの良い例である。ビデオ／映画制作を教育や研究に取り入れることは、文字と映像の境界線を崩し、本質化、カテゴリー化、二項対立化に抵抗し挑戦する新たな考え方を研究者／教育者と学習者が生み出す上で役に立つ。また、フィルム－イング実践の場合、学習者の英語力とクリティカル・メディアリテラシーの強化を促進する。リンガ・フランカ（共通語）としての英語の世界での普及に注目し、Kachru (2006) は、「現代の英語には唯一の定義状況があるのではなく、さまざまな文化および言語にまたがって多様な状況がある」(p.275) と述べた。そのような状況の中で、英語を用いた多様な表現方法を奨励する必要がある。Kubota (2004) は、「批判的な多文化教育」の実践の必要性にふれ、教師と生徒の双方に望まれる姿勢を以下のように述べている。

> ヨーロッパ中心の規範への同化は、多様性についての表面的な称賛の基礎となることがしばしばあり、世界観や言語形態の多様化を妨げていることを認識する必要がある。正真正銘の多元的共存および多様性をはっきりと主張するには、さまざまな考え方や言語形態のヒエラルキーを維持している現存の権力関係に疑問を投げかけ、対抗する言説に向けた可能性を探ることが必要である。(pp.45–46)

フィルム－イング実践は、ここで論じられている真の多様性の出現に貢献するものである。

　先述のように、授業におけるビデオ／映画制作実施を成功させるためには、クリティカル・メディアリテラシーの育成が不可欠である。Luke (2014) によると、この新たなタイプのリテラシーは、「公共施設や日常生活の社会的な部分を管理している規範、規則制度、慣例を分析し、批評

し、変える」(p.21) ために必要である。クリティカル・メディアリテラシーを身につけることで、生徒たちは多様なメッセージを解読し、新たな考えを発信できる高度な能力を持った活動的な地球市民になり、より公正な世界の実現に貢献することができる。

　さらに、フィルム－イング実践は 21 世紀において若い世代が自身の未来を切り拓くのに必要な批判的思考とアクティブ・ラーニングを促進する。Shohat & Stam (1994) は、視聴覚教材による指導の導入には大きな効果があるとしている。彼らはその指導法を「視聴覚教授法」(p.10) と呼び、この教授法は「生徒自身の観念的な思い込みや感情的投資に注意を促すため、教室自体の社会的な多様性を展開する」(p.357) と説明している。教育におけるオーディオとビジュアルの活用は、生徒の批判的思考を高め、国家・人種・民族・ジェンダー等に関する多様性への気付きと肯定につながる。それゆえに批判的思考は、学習者が自身を取り巻く状況を認識し、より大きなコンテクストに自分自身を結びつけて考え、さらには、考えを行動に変える助けとなる。このように、教育における批判的思考の涵養は必要不可欠であるといえる。

　さらに、アクティブ・ラーニングは、教師と生徒に対し、銀行型教育を起源とする伝統的な指導・学習法を超えるよう促す。この新たな教育方法を授業で実践するには、教師と生徒の双方ができるだけ努力する必要がある。生徒たちの自主性を促すため、指導者は柔軟性を持ち、ファシリテーターとしての役割を果たし、教室内にポジティブな勇気づける環境を作ることが求められる。学習者は、住み慣れた居心地の良い場所から出て、自身の意見を述べながらも異なる考えに耳を傾ける必要がある。教育者も学生も多様性が承認される寛容な共有空間をはぐくむ義務がある。教師の努力と学習者の努力が重なり合ったとき、「真の学習コミュニティー」(Barkley, 2010, p.125) が誕生する。Meyers & Jones (1993) は、「自己の学びに責任を持つようになる学生たちは、我々の社会をより民主的で、万人にとってより良い場所にする助けとなるだろう」(p.17) と述べ、アクティブ・ラーニングの効果をまとめている。

本書では、フィルム-イング実践を提示しつつ、さまざまな教育の場で多様な芸術様式を使用することを提唱し、学者や学生がアートを用いた独創的で型にはまらない作品を作り出すことの意義について述べた。アートベース実践の教育への導入により、指導者と学習者に規範、つまり、当然だと思われていることに疑問を投げかける自由が与えられる。Leavy (2015) が「アートベース実践は、方法論の最前線にあり、研究者たちは新たな実践を切り開き、新たな見方を生んでいる」(p.291、強調は原文) と述べたように、アートベース・アプローチの実践者は、大きな可能性を握っていると筆者は信じている。

　本書を締めくくる前に、ここで指導者／研究者の責務を強調しておきたい。それについて、Barone & Eisner (2012) は、次のように明確に表現している。

　　……映画を用いることのできる能力は、世界あるいはその様相を描き、理解するための重要な力の一つであることは確実だろう。表象形態における加速する多様化の結果として、大学やその他の機関において、有益なことを成すのに必要な技能および才能を持つ個々の研究者を用意する必要性が出てくるだろう。［中略］ビデオテープが、ある話や出来事の詳細な状況を伝える強力な手段となるのであれば、映像を扱う者には、それを有効に用いる能力が必要となる。(p.169)

このようにアートベース実践者は、技能の熟練者でかつ革新的、しかも異なる価値観に対して寛大であるべきである。本書で強調したいのは、映像制作従事者は、権威・権力・視線・表象の問題を考慮に入れる必要があるということである。同時に、意図したメッセージを視聴者がさまざまに解釈するということに留意することが映像制作者にとって重要である。Hickman (2007) は、この点について次のように説明している。

　　アートベース・アプローチは、データ収集の段階と報告の段階で用いることができるが、後者では、視聴者（あるいはむしろ観客）が映像を解

釈するのにあまり慣れていない可能性があり、視聴者の解釈により複雑さが加わる。しかし、「アーティスト」はアート作品の中で生み出されたすべてのものの複雑性や豊かさ、隠れた意味に必ずしも気付いているわけではないため、これは強みとして捉えることもできる。(p.316)

Hickman がここで述べているように、新しい知識を生み出し、共有する革新的な方法は、アートベース実践者と観客との相互作用から生まれるのである。

　フィルム－イング実践を通じて、筆者は、読者に各々の教育の場において、アートベース・アプローチを実践することを奨励する。特に映像制作を行うためには、批判的な視点を持ち続けることが必要不可欠であり、そうすることにより、映像制作者はメッセージの送信者として規範に挑み、新たな考え方を提案することができると信じる。Chan (2008) は、世界における社会正義の実現に向けて励んでいる、日本在住の活発な地球市民について次のように言及している。

本書のタイトル『もう一つの日本は可能だ』は、日本におけるオルター・グローバリゼーションの活動家のスローガンおよび思想を反映しており、彼らは、世界中に広がったより大きな地球レベルでの正義運動の重要な要素であり、もう一つの世界は可能であるという信念のもと結集している。[中略] その運動は、透明性、民主主義、参加にもとづく新たなグローバリゼーションの形を目指している。(p. 17、強調は原文)

日本の若者たちには無限の可能性がある。生まれ育った文化・言語について深く理解し、英語とデジタル技術を駆使する能力を獲得することで、彼らは活発な地球市民となり、新たな考えを生み出すことが可能になる。今こそ若いデジタル世代が批判的かつ活動的になり、アートベース実践の準備を整え、文化的な起源 (roots) および今後進む道筋 (routes) の両方を見つめ、自己表現を行うときである。

References

Anderson, N., Duncan, B., & Pungente, J. (2001). Media education, Canadian stories. *Australian Screen Education, 25,* 32–39.

Barkley, E. (2010). *Student engagement techniques: A handbook for college faculty.* San Francisco, CA: Jossey-Bass.

Barone, T., & Eisner, E. (2012). *Arts based research.* Thousand Oaks, CA: Sage.

Bean, J. (2011). *Engaging ideas: The Professor's guide to integrating writing, critical thinking, and active learning in the classroom* (2nd ed.). San Francisco, CA: Jossey-Bass.

Chan, J. (Ed.). (2008). *Another Japan is possible: New social movements and global citizenship education.* Stanford, CA: Stanford University Press.

Chauvin, B. A. (2003). Visual or media literacy? *Journal of Visual Literacy, 23* (2), 119–128.

Dewey, J. (1934). *Art as experience.* New York, NY: Minton, Balch & Company.

Doane, M. (1982). Film and the masquerade: Theorising the female spectator. *Screen, 23* (3–4), 74–87.

Duffelmeyer, B. (2004). Visualizing *respect*: Visual media literacy and students' understanding of globalization and technology issues. *Journal of Visual Literacy, 24* (2), 165–184.

Duncan, B. (2005). Media literacy: Essential survival skills for the new millennium. *Orbit, 35* (2), 2–4.

Dyer, R. (1993). *The matter of images: Essays on representations.* New York, NY: Routledge.

Eisner, E. (1972). *Educating artistic vision.* New York, NY: Macmillan.

Eisner, E. (2002). *Arts and the creation of mind.* New Haven, CT: Yale University Press.

Ellsworth, E. (1997). *Teaching positions: Difference, pedagogy, and the power of address.* New York, NY: Teachers College Press.

Flaherty, R. (Producer). (1976). *Nanook of the north* [Motion picture]. United States: Janus Films. (Original film produced 1922)

Frank, L. (1966). Role of the arts in education. In E. Eisner & D. Ecker (Eds.), *Readings in art education* (pp. 454–459). Toronto, Canada: Xerox College Publishing.

Freire, P. (2003). *Pedagogy of the oppressed.* New York, NY: Continuum. (Original work published 1970)

Fukuda, H. (2003). *Jazz up your Japanese with onomatopoeia: For all levels.* Tokyo, Japan: Kodansha International.

Goldberg, M. (2001). *Arts and learning: An integrated approach to teaching and learning in multicultural and multilingual settings.* New York, NY: Addison Wesley Longman.

Goodlad, J., & Morrison, J. (1980). The arts and education. In J. Hausman (Ed.), *Arts and the schools* (pp. 1–21). New York, NY: McGraw-Hill Book Company.

Hall, S. (1999). Encoding, decoding. In S. During (Ed.), *The cultural studies reader* (2nd ed., pp. 507–517). New York, NY: Routledge. (Original work published 1980)

Hara, H. (2014). Confronting media representation: Cambodian diaspora and self-expression as counter-narrative. *The Bulletin of Ikuei Junior College, 31*, 29–43.

Hara, H. (Producer). (2015). *Yugen* [DVD]. Japan: Hara Pekkori Girls Productions.

Hara, H. (2016). Arts-Based research in practice: Towards a new mode of address across harmony and disharmony. *The Bulletin of Ikuei Junior College, 33*, 1–11.

Hartley, J. (2007). "There are other ways of being in the truth": The uses of multimedia literacy. *International Journal of Cultural Studies, 10* (1), 135–144.

Hickman, R. (2007). Visual art as a vehicle for educational research. *Journal of Art and Design Education (JADE) 26* (3), 314–324.

hooks, b. (2003). *Teaching community: A pedagogy of hope.* New York, NY: Routledge.

Ippolito, J. (2007). From the avant-garde: Re-Conceptualizing cultural origins in the digital media art of Japan. *Leonardo, 40* (2), 142–151.

Ivers, K., & Barron, A. (2006). *Multimedia projects in education: Designing, producing, and assessing.* Westport, CT: Libraries Unlimited.

Kachru, B. (2006). The alchemy of English. In B. Ashcroft, G. Griffiths, & H. Tiffin (Eds.), *The post-colonial studies reader* (2nd ed., pp. 272–275). New York, NY: Routledge.

Kindon, S. (2003). Participatory video in geographic research: A feminist practice of looking? *Area, 35* (2), 142–153.

Kubota, R. (2004). Critical multiculturalism and second language education. In B. Norton & K. Toohey (Eds.), *Critical pedagogies and language learning* (pp. 30–52). Cambridge, United Kingdom: Cambridge University Press.

Kusama, Y. (2002). *Mugen no ami: Kusama Yayoi jiden* [Infinity net: The autobiography of Yayoi Kusama]. Tokyo, Japan: Shinchosha.

Kusama, Y. (2011). *Infinity net: The autobiography of Yayoi Kusama* (R. McCarthy, Trans.). Chicago, IL: University of Chicago Press.

Lankshear, C., & Knobel, M. (2005). Paulo Freire and digital youth in marginal spaces. In G. Fischman, P. McLaren, H. Sünker, & C. Lankshear (Eds.), *Critical theories, radical pedagogies, and global conflicts* (pp. 293–306). Lanham, MD: Rowman & Littlefield.

Leavy, P. (2015). *Method meets art: Arts-Based research practice* (2nd ed.). New York, NY: The Guilford Press.

Lewis, H. (1976). Crystal gazing, forecasting, and wishful thinking: The future of the arts in public education. In E. Eisner (Ed.), *The arts, human development, and education* (pp. 159–173). Berkeley, CA: McCutchan Publishing.

Loutzenheiser, L. (2005). Working fluidity, materiality and the educational imaginary: A case for contingent primacy. *Journal of the Canadian Association for Curriculum Studies, 3* (2), 27–39.

Luke, A. (2014). Defining critical literacy. In J. Pandya & J. Ávila (Eds.), *Moving critical literacies forward: A new look at praxis across contexts* (pp. 19–31). New York, NY: Routledge.

MacDougall, D. (2006). *The corporeal image: Film, ethnography, and the senses*. Princeton, NJ: Princeton University Press.

Mayhall, Y. (1989). *The sumi-e book*. New York, NY: Watson-Guptill.

McLuhan, M. (1988a). Inside on the outside, or the spaced-out American. *Antigonish Review, 74–75*, 144–152.

McLuhan, M. (1988b). The role of new media in social change. *Antigonish Review, 74–75*, 43–49.

Meyers, C., & Jones, T. (1993). *Promoting active learning: Strategies for the college classroom*. San Francisco, CA: Jossey-Bass.

Miller, K., & Zhou, X. (2007). Learning from classroom video: What makes it compelling and what makes it hard. In R. Goldman, R. Pea, B. Barron, & S. Derry (Eds.), *Video research in the learning sciences* (pp. 321–334). Mahwah, NJ: Lawrence Erlbaum.

Millerson, G. (2001). *Video production handbook* (3rd ed.). Oxford, United Kingdom: Focal Press.

Millerson, G., & Owens, J. (2009). *Television production* (14th ed.). Oxford, United Kingdom: Focal Press.

Millington, S. (1993). *Nihongo pera pera!: A user's guide to Japanese onomatopoeia*. Rutland, VT: Charles E. Tuttle Publishing.

Ministry of Education, Culture, Sports, Science and Technology. (2011). *The vision for ICT in education: Toward the creation of a learning system and schools suitable for the 21st century*. Retrieved September 3, 2017, from http://www.mext.go.jp/component/a_menu/education/micro_detail/__icsFiles/afieldfile/2017/06/26/1305484_14_1.pdf

Ministry of Education, Culture, Sports, Science and Technology. (2013a). *The second basic plan for the promotion of education* (provisional translation). Retrieved September 3, 2017, from http://www.mext.go.jp/en/policy/education/lawandplan/title01/detail01/1373796.htm

Ministry of Education, Culture, Sports, Science and Technology. (2013b). *White paper on education, culture, sports, science and technology*. Retrieved September 3, 2017, from http://www.mext.go.jp/b_menu/hakusho/html/hpab201301/detail/1360673.htm

Ministry of Education, Culture, Sports, Science and Technology. (2013c).

References

English education reform plan corresponding to globalization. Retrieved September 3, 2017, from http://www.mext.go.jp/en/news/topics/detail/__icsFiles/afieldfile/2014/01/23/1343591_1.pdf

Mirzoeff, N. (1998). What is visual culture? In N. Mirzoeff (Ed.), *The visual culture reader* (pp. 3–13). New York, NY: Routledge.

Mitchell, C. (2016). Autoethnography as a wide-angle lens on looking (inward and outward): What difference can this make to our teaching? In D. Pillay, I. Naicker, & K. Pithouse-Morgan (Eds.), *Academic autoethnographies: Inside teaching in higher education* (pp. 175–189). Rotterdam, The Netherlands: Sense.

Moletsane, R., Mitchell, C., & Lewin, T. (2015). Gender violence, teenage pregnancy and gender equity policy in South Africa: Privileging the voices of women and girls through participatory visual methods. In J. Parkes (Ed.), *Gender violence in poverty contexts: The educational challenge* (pp. 183–196). New York, NY: Routledge.

Naito, H. (2016, October 31). Foreign visitors to Japan top 20 million for first time in 2016. *The Asahi Shimbun.* Retrieved September 3, 2017, from http://www.asahi.com/ajw/articles/AJ201610310055.html

National Institution for Youth Education. (2015). *Kōkōsei no seikatsu to ishiki ni kansuru chōsa hōkokusho* [Report of survey on high school students' views on life]. Retrieved September 3, 2017, from http://www.niye.go.jp/kanri/upload/editor/98/File/05.2.pdf

Ngũgĩ, T. (1986). *Decolonising the mind: The politics of language in African literature.* London, United Kingdom: James Currey.

Okamoto, N. (2015). *The art of sumi-e: Beautiful ink painting using Japanese brushwork.* Kent, United Kingdom: Search Press.

Ontario Ministry of Education. (2006). *The Ontario curriculum, grades 1–8: Language.* Retrieved September 2, 2017, from http://www.edu.gov.on.ca/eng/curriculum/elementary/language18currb.pdf

Ontario Ministry of Education. (2007a). *The Ontario curriculum, grades 1–8: Science and technology.* Retrieved September 2, 2017, from http://www.edu.gov.on.ca/eng/curriculum/elementary/scientec18currb.pdf

Ontario Ministry of Education. (2007b). *The Ontario curriculum, grades 9 and 10: English*. Retrieved September 2, 2017, from http://www.edu.gov. on.ca/eng/curriculum/secondary/english910currb.pdf

Ontario Ministry of Education. (2007c). *The Ontario curriculum, grades 11 and 12: English*. Retrieved September 2, 2017, from http://www.edu.gov. on.ca/eng/curriculum/secondary/english1112currb.pdf

Ontario Ministry of Education. (2009a). *The Ontario curriculum, grades 9 and 10: Technological education*. Retrieved September 2, 2017, from http://www.edu.gov.on.ca/eng/curriculum/secondary/teched910curr09.pdf

Ontario Ministry of Education. (2009b). *The Ontario curriculum, grades 1–8: The arts*. Retrieved September 2, 2017, from http://www.edu.gov. on.ca/eng/curriculum/elementary/arts18b09curr.pdf

Ontario Ministry of Education. (2009c). *The Ontario curriculum, grades 11 and 12: Technological education*. Retrieved September 2, 2017, from http://www.edu.gov.on.ca/eng/curriculum/secondary/2009teched1112curr.pdf

Ontario Ministry of Education. (2010a). *The Ontario curriculum, grades 9 and 10: The arts*. Retrieved September 2, 2017, from http://www.edu.gov. on.ca/eng/curriculum/secondary/arts910curr2010.pdf

Ontario Ministry of Education. (2010b). *The Ontario curriculum, grades 11 and 12: The arts*. Retrieved September 2, 2017, from http://www.edu.gov. on.ca/eng/curriculum/secondary/arts1112curr2010.pdf

Palys, T. (2003). *Research decisions: Quantitative and qualitative perspectives* (3rd ed.). Scarborough, Canada: Nelson.

Pharr, S. (1996). Media and politics in Japan: Historical and contemporary perspectives. In S. Pharr and E. Krauss (Eds.), *Media and politics in Japan* (pp. 3–17). Honolulu, HI: University of Hawaii Press.

Pink, S. (2007). *Doing visual ethnography: Images, media and representation in research*. London, United Kingdom: Sage.

Pogue, D. (2006). *iMovie 6 & iDVD: The missing manual*. Sebastopol, CA: O'Reilly Media.

Prime Minister of Japan and His Cabinet. (2014). *Japan revitalization strategy: Japan's challenge for the future*. Retrieved September 3, 2017, from http://www.kantei.go.jp/jp/singi/keizaisaisei/pdf/honbunEN.pdf

References

Prince, M. (2004). Does active learning work?: A review of the research. *Journal of Engineering Education, 93* (3), 223–231.

Ragains, P. (2006). Setting the stage for information literacy education. In P. Ragains (Ed.), *Information literacy instruction that works: A guide to teaching by discipline and student population* (pp. 3–17). New York, NY: Neal-Schuman.

Reed, W. (1989). *Shodo: The art of coordinating mind, body and brush.* Tokyo, Japan: Japan Publications.

Russell, C. (1999). *Experimental ethnography.* Durham, NC: Duke University Press.

Semali, L. (2000). *Literacy in multimedia America: Integrating media education across the curriculum.* New York, NY: Falmer Press.

Shohat, E., & Stam, R. (1994). *Unthinking Eurocentrism: Multiculturalism and the media.* New York, NY: Routledge.

Siegesmund, R., & Cahnmann-Taylor, M. (2008). The tensions of arts-based research in education reconsidered: The promise for practice. In M. Cahnmann-Taylor & R. Siegesmund (Eds.), *Arts-Based research in education: Foundations for practice* (pp. 231–246). New York, NY: Routledge.

Strategic Headquarters for the Promotion of an Advanced Information and Telecommunications Network Society. (2009). *i-Japan strategy 2015: Striving to create a citizen-driven, reassuring & vibrant digital society.* Retrieved September 3, 2017, from http://japan.kantei.go.jp/policy/it/i-JapanStrategy2015_full.pdf

Strategic Headquarters for the Promotion of an Advanced Information and Telecommunications Network Society. (2013). *Declaration to be the world's most advanced IT nation.* Retrieved September 3, 2017, from http://japan.kantei.go.jp/policy/it/2013/0614_declaration.pdf

Tannenbaum, M., & Goldstein, A. (2005). Multiliteracies as a bridge between the curriculum and the individual: On teaching art via the personal photo album. *Journal of Visual Literacy, 25* (2), 123–144.

Trinh, T. M. (1991). *When the moon waxes red: Representation, gender and cultural politics.* New York, NY: Routledge.

Trinh, T. M. (1999). *Cinema interval*. New York, NY: Routledge.
Trinh, T. M. (2013). *D-Passage: The digital way*. Durham, NC: Duke University Press.
Tyner, K. (2003). Beyond boxes and wires: Literacy in transition. *Television & New Media, 4* (4), 371–388.
Walter, P. (1999). Defining literacy and its consequences in the developing world. *International Journal of Lifelong Education, 18* (1), 31–48.
Zeami. (2005). *Gendaigoyaku* Fushikaden [A contemporary Japanese translation of the *Fushikaden*] (S. Mizuno, Trans.). Tokyo, Japan: PHP.
Zeami. (2006). *The spirit of noh: A new translation of the classic noh treatise the* Fushikaden (W. Wilson, Trans.). Boston, MA: Shambhala.

Index

active learning, 8, 17, 30–34, 84–85
angles, 35, 40–41, 46, 51, 57
art, 4–5, 7, 16–17, 75, 81–82, 85–86
arts-based, 5, 8, 83, 85–87, 97
arts-based education, 4, 8, 82, 84, 86, 90
arts-based research, 6, 82
audience, 8, 26–29, 37–39, 41–42, 50, 52, 54–55, 57, 70, 75–80, 86
authority, 27, 29, 86
Barkley, Elizabeth, 30, 33, 59, 85, 120, 123, 141
Barone, Tom, 5–7, 82, 85, 97–98, 161, 164
Bean, John, 30, 33, 50, 120, 123, 136
binary, 5, 29, 70–71
boundaries, 5, 18
calligraphy, 68–69
Chan, Jennifer, 87, 165
Chauvin, B. A., 11, 102
concept of *yugen*, 68–70
constructivism, 22
critical media literacy, 7–13, 24–25, 32–33, 76, 83–84
critical thinking, 12, 19, 22–26, 33, 49, 84
culture, vii, 2–4, 11, 13, 20, 68–72, 74, 81, 87
decoding, 7–8, 26–27, 29, 50, 68, 75, 84
Dewey, John, 4–5, 95–96
digitalization, 8, 10–11, 13, 16–17, 24
diversity, 6, 48, 50, 83–85

Doane, Mary, 29, 118–19
Duffelmeyer, Barb, 11, 102
Duncan, Barry, 20, 111
Dyer, Richard, 48, 134
editing, 8, 41–43, 45–47, 49, 60, 74
Eisner, Elliot, 4–7, 82, 85, 95–98, 161, 164
Ellsworth, Elizabeth, 75, 78–79, 155, 158
encoding, 7–8, 26, 29–31, 33, 35, 37, 39, 41, 43–47, 50, 68, 75, 84
English language skills, 7, 11, 13–14, 83
ethnicity, 8, 26, 32–33, 84
ethnographic film, 27
ethnography, 27
feminist film theory, 28
film techniques, 8, 35, 46, 49, 51, 56–57, 68
Film-Eng praxis, 7–8, 13, 31, 34, 49–51, 53, 55–57, 59–60, 68, 74, 83–84, 86, 98
filming, 7–8, 26, 28, 34–37, 40–42, 44–47, 49, 60–61, 98
filmmaker, ix, 8, 28–29, 44, 47–48, 75–76, 78–80, 86–87
filmmaking, 7, 47–48, 83, 86–87
Frank, Lawrence, 4, 95–96
Freire, Paulo, 23, 31, 49, 114, 121, 135
Fukuda, Hiroko, 72, 152
gaze, 28–29, 32, 86
gender, 8, 23, 26, 32–33, 48, 78, 84

175

global citizen(s), vii–viii, 84, 87, 90
globalization, 8, 10–13, 17, 24, 87
Goldberg, Merryl, 81–82, 160–61
Hall, Stuart, 8, 26, 75, 99, 116, 155
hand-held camera, 35
Hara, Hiroko, 26, 28, 61, 63–64, 66–67, 83, 116, 118, 143, 162
Hartley, John, 12, 103
Hickman, Richard, 5, 82, 86, 97, 161, 164–65
hooks, bell, 23–24, 114
ICT literacy, 14–15, 17, 21–23
ICT skills, viii, 14, 16, 18–19, 30
image, viii, 2, 24, 28, 36, 38, 44, 46–48, 51, 54–55, 68, 70, 76, 78, 83, 86
Ippolito, Jean, 16, 107
Japanese language, vii, 72
Kachru, Braj, 83, 162
Kindon, Sara, 47, 133
knowledge, 7, 12, 15, 17–19, 22–23, 31, 48–51, 78, 82, 86
Kubota, Ryuko, 83, 162
Kusama, Yayoi, vii, 81, 89, 160
language, vii–viii, 7, 10–11, 13–14, 18–19, 21, 27, 71–74, 77, 82–83, 87
Leavy, Patricia, 5–6, 82, 85, 97, 161, 164
Lewis, Hilda, 4–5, 95–96
lighting, 35, 41
literacies, 7, 10–11, 13, 19, 21, 23, 32
Loutzenheiser, Lisa, 48, 134
Luke, Allan, 84, 162
MacDougall, David, 27, 117
Mayhall, Yolanda, 70, 150
McLuhan, Marshall, 18, 20, 109, 111
media education in Canada, 18–21

media education in Japan, 13–15, 17, 22
media literacy, 3, 7–13, 19–21, 24–25, 32–33, 76, 83–84
Millerson, Gerald, 42, 44, 128, 130
Millington, Susan, 72, 153
Ministry of Education, Culture, Sports, Science and Technology (MEXT), 3–4, 10, 12, 15, 17, 30
Mirzoeff, Nicholas, 3, 94
Mitchell, Claudia, 3, 95
Naito, Hisashi, 34, 124
Nanook of the North (Flaherty), 27
National Institution for Youth Education, 3
Ngũgĩ, wa Thiong'o, 71, 152
Okamoto, Naomi, 69, 150
onomatopoeia, 72, 77
Ontario Ministry of Education (OME), 18–21, 109–12
panning, 37–38, 46
Pharr, Susan, 14, 105
Pink, Sarah, 28, 118
Pogue, David, 41–42, 128
power, 19, 21, 23, 26, 29, 31–32, 47–48, 70, 82, 84, 86
Prime Minister of Japan and His Cabinet, 10
Prince, Michael, 30, 120
race, 8, 23, 26, 32–33, 48, 78, 84
Ragains, Patrick, 11, 102
Reed, William, 70, 151
representation, 6, 28, 32, 47, 86
rhythm, 61, 68, 73–74
Russell, Catherine, 27–28, 117–18
Semali, Ladislaus, 24, 115

Index

sound, viii, 35, 42, 45–47, 51–52, 54–55, 73
storyboard, 44–46, 51–57, 59–60
storyboarding, 7–8, 44–45, 49, 51–52, 56–57
storytelling, 68, 70, 72–73
Strategic Headquarters for the Promotion of an Advanced Information and Telecommunications Network Society (IT Strategic Headquarters), 14–16
technology, 2–4, 11–12, 14, 16–18, 21–22, 81, 87
tilting, 37–38, 46
Trinh, T. Minh-ha, 2, 48, 69–70, 73, 76, 79–80, 94, 134, 150–51, 153, 156–59
tripod use, 35
Tyner, Kathleen, 11, 22–23, 102, 113–14
types of shots, 35, 38, 41, 46, 51, 57
visual culture, 2–3, 11, 81
Walter, Pierre, 12, 102
Zeami, 68–69, 75, 149, 155
zooming, 36, 38, 46

About the Author

Hiroko Hara received a M.A. and a Ph.D. in Educational Studies from the University of British Columbia (Canada). She is currently a senior lecturer at the Department of English Language and Literature at the Prefectural University of Kumamoto. Her research interests include visual culture, intercultural communication, film theory and production, and postcolonial theory.

From April 2017 to present: Senior Lecturer at the Department of English Language and Literature at the Prefectural University of Kumamoto.

From April 2013 to March 2017: Senior Lecturer at the Department of Communication, Ikuei College in Gunma.

Arts-Based Education to Become Global Citizens
地球市民となるためのアートベース教育

2018年3月16日　初版発行

著　者　　原　　　紘子

発行者　　福岡　正人

発行所　　株式会社　金　星　堂

（〒101-0051）東京都千代田区神田神保町 3-21
　　　　　　　Tel. (03)3263-3828（営業部）
　　　　　　　　　(03)3263-3997（編集部）
　　　　　　　Fax (03)3263-0716
　　　　　　　http://www.kinsei-do.co.jp

組版／ほんのしろ
印刷所／興亜産業　製本所／松島製本
落丁・乱丁本はお取り替えいたします
本書の内容を無断で複写・複製することを禁じます
©2018 Hiroko Hara　Printed in Japan
ISBN978-4-7647-1182-2 C3082